# OPPORTUNITIES

in

# Arts and Crafts Careers

## REVISED EDITION

D0974935

## Elizabeth B. Gardner

## McGraw·Hill

New York   Chicago   San Francisco   Lisbon   London   Madrid   Mexico City
Milan   New Delhi   San Juan   Seoul   Singapore   Sydney   Toronto

Library of Congress Cataloging-in-Publication Data

Gardner, Elizabeth B.
    Opportunities in arts and crafts careers / Elizabeth B. Gardner. — Rev. ed.
        p.    cm.
    ISBN 0-07-144849-7
    1. Arts—Vocational guidance.    2. Handicraft—Vocational guidance.
  I. Title.

    NX163.G37    2006
    700'.23—dc22                            2005005109

2 3 4 5 6 7 8 9 0   DOC/DOC   0 9 8 7 6 5

ISBN 0-07-144849-7

Interior design by Rattray Design

McGraw-Hill books are available at special quantity discounts to use as premiums and sales promotions, or for use in corporate training programs. For more information, please write to the Director of Special Sales, Professional Publishing, McGraw-Hill, Two Penn Plaza, New York, NY 10121-2298. Or contact your local bookstore.

This book is printed on acid-free paper.

# Contents

# PREFACE

WHEN WE TALK about art, we are often referring to what tradition-ally are known as the fine arts—painting, sculpture, drawing, and so forth. But the term art offers a much broader description in that it involves skill in making or doing something. Thus the umbrella of art also covers photography, architecture, weaving, ceramics, and much more. The distinction between what is an art and what is a craft is often blurred as many artistic works can be considered both.

All of the arts presented in this book require talent and skill. If you are one of those individuals who possess the necessary talent and acquire the necessary skills, *Opportunities in Arts and Crafts Careers* can help you get started on an exciting and fulfilling career doing what you love to do.

# ACKNOWLEDGMENTS

I AM GRATEFUL to the following individuals for their help in the preparation of this book: John Bellian, David Berry, Kathy Burden, Michael Cookinham, Ann Corcoran, Ann Gardner, Janet Gardner, Jean Gardner, Owen Gardner, Joel Greenberg, Leo Holub Sr., Ananda Kavana, Ka Kavana, Ted Laird, Julie Lockman, Moira McClintock, Cheryl Miller, Brenda Palley, Carole Rae, Eleanore Ramsey, Patricia Rose, Paul Ryan, Pearl Stevens, James Stevenson, and Suzanne Tucker. Their generosity in sharing their expertise made this book possible.

# 1

# ARCHITECTURE

SOME STRUCTURES CONCEIVED by architects endure for thousands of years. Forty-seven hundred years ago the architect Imhotep erected a stepped pyramid for the Egyptian pharaoh Zoser. This pyramid still stands, the first large structure built of stone of which we have any knowledge. Viewed from afar, the pyramid's six giant steps look like a stairway to the stars, the whole a monument to eternity.

The oldest buildings we know anything about were erected three thousand years ago in Asia Minor, Egypt, and Greece. Some of these temples survive in part. A Grecian temple consisted of a walled rectangle bordered by stone columns that supported beams on which a gabled roof rested. Each temple provided shelter for an image of a god or goddess.

## History of Architecture

Sometime during the first millennium before Christ, the Etruscans developed the arch, a means of spanning the distance between two supports with small stones or bricks. By extension, the arch made possible vaults. With vaults, builders could roof huge spaces without intervening columns. The Romans employed the arch and vault to build their monumental constructions—viaducts, baths, and arenas such as the Colosseum in Rome.

After 1000 A.D., the Romanesque style continued the use of the arch and vault, principally in churches. Romanesque architecture scattered throughout Western Europe and Italy varies from region to region, providing fascinating interpretations of the Roman architecture whose remains still grace the landscape.

In the 1100s, French master builders started using buttresses aligned with interior piers to help transfer the weight of vaults to the ground. Strain on the outer walls thus was lessened, making it possible to pierce the walls with great stained-glass windows. Through these windows, magical light streams into the vast, vaulted spaces. Local clergy and their fellow townspeople constructed Gothic cathedrals on these principles throughout Europe, mostly during the next hundred years or so.

Toward the end of the nineteenth century, builders started using steel and concrete reinforced with steel. Previously stone, wood, and brick served as the usual building materials. The use of steel made possible the tall buildings once aptly called skyscrapers but now called high-rises. Reinforced concrete made possible buildings in shapes that otherwise would be impossible to construct. These new methods led to streamlining—a striving for simplicity and efficiency and a doing away with surface decoration. The German-born Mies van der Rohe explained the goal in his dictum "Less is more." The new materials and the new outlook led to what we call modern architecture.

In recent years, a movement away from the austerity of modern architecture developed in response to a feeling that the clean, sweeping lines of modern architecture leave something to be desired, that the human soul craves the delights of ornamentation. An American architect, Robert Venturi, expressed this sentiment as "Less is boring." As a result, a postmodernist style, which returned to the use of ornamentation, came into being.

In the late 1980s, some architects abandoned modernism and postmodernism and began designing buildings in a style that has been labeled *deconstructivism*, which seeks a departure from previous forms. To accomplish this goal, deconstructivist architects design buildings with skewed geometry—slanting walls, twisted structures, windows whose alignment is staggered rather than placed in a precise horizontal band, moldings that waver across the facade—almost anything that is in opposition to the traditional design. An example of a deconstructionist building is the curvaceous, titanium-clad Guggenheim Museum in Bilbao, Spain, which received considerable publicity when it opened in 1997. This building was designed by Frank Gehry, who with Peter Eisenman and Richard Meier are the principal exponents of this style.

At the same time, while some architects remain true to the postmodernist ideal, other architects are returning to modernism. What the future will bring in the way of architectural styles remains to be seen.

## What Architects Do

Most often, an architect's client already owns a building site. If not, the architect helps the client find a suitable site. The design the architect develops must use the site to the best advantage. Also, in developing a design, the architect takes into consideration how the building will relate to neighboring buildings. Making a building compatible with its surroundings doesn't imply that the architect designs the new building in the same style as other buildings in the neighborhood. Copying the work of other architects constitutes a breach of ethics, and copying the architecture of another era seems inappropriate. An architect must design for today, as our ways of living and doing things differ from those of peoples of the past. Also, new methods of building and new materials become available. New buildings should reflect these realities. A building appropriate for its site, even though its architecture departs from the style of its neighbors, harmonizes with them in size and materials.

A good architect ranks as an artist of the highest caliber, for the buildings he or she designs please aesthetically. Their good looks result from consideration of a number of factors. The relationships of parts to each other and to the whole with respect to size perhaps constitute the most important consideration. Attention to proportions includes regard for such relationships as height to width, solid wall to window and door openings, one section of a building to another. The materials, colors, textures, repetition of forms for rhythmic effect, balance—whether symmetrical or asymmetrical—and an agreeable relationship among these elements all contribute to the pleasing appearance of a building.

A good architect designs buildings that not only please aesthetically but are also structurally sound. To this end, architectural students learn the principles of engineering, and practicing architects keep their knowledge of construction methods up-to-date.

To succeed financially, an architect operates his or her office in a businesslike manner and manages to deal satisfactorily with clients, office staff, contractors, and others. Of course, an architect can delegate some duties, such as office procedures to a business manager. An architect also often seeks the collaboration of outside specialists on matters such as foundations and soils, electrical systems, plumbing systems, bathrooms, kitchens, landscaping, or other matters related to building. The architect coordinates the work of specialists, so that plans combine to give the client the best possible building for his or her money.

The architect's prime responsibility is the creation of a design for a building appropriate for its purpose, location, and time. To arrive at such a design, the architect discusses with the client the activities that will take place in the building and from this information devises a floor plan to fulfill those needs, not necessarily sticking to "tried-and-true" arrangements but exercising ingenuity to arrive at even better solutions.

In planning a building, an architect gives attention to many details: movement of people in and out and up and down; air conditions (ventilation, heating, cooling, and humidity control); lighting, both natural and artificial; water supply and sanitation; sound reduction or enhancement; safety and security; and more. Also, the cost of the building must not exceed the client's budget.

During the planning stage, an architect sometimes makes a small-scale, three-dimensional model of the proposed building. A model gives the client a clearer picture of the architect's proposal than drawings do; it also serves as an aid to the architect in determining the best spatial arrangement. A model also often shows the topography of the site, the placement of the building on the property, and the suggested landscaping. Sometimes the architect delegates the job of building the model either to someone else in the office or to a firm specializing in model building. A model can be made with the help of a computer program called CAD (Computer Aided Design).

Once the architect and any assistants formulate the plans, they go over them again and again to ensure that they represent the best possible solution and that no errors exist. Even so, during the construction process, changes sometimes become necessary due to material, manufacturing, and/or supply problems.

Once the plans satisfy both client and architect, the architect prepares specifications that indicate the materials and building methods to be used. The architect also prepares working drawings that show where each part of the building goes and that include details such as the electrical, plumbing, and any mechanical systems.

The architect gives copies of the specifications and working drawings to prospective contractors. The contractors then submit bids, which are statements of their proposed charges. In some cases, a contractor takes a job on a cost-plus-fee basis. This means the contractor's remuneration equals the cost of materials and labor plus a predetermined fee.

With growth in population, the demand for architects will increase. A greater population will make necessary new housing, schools, hospitals, nursing homes, churches, office buildings, industrial plants, stores, hotels, restaurants, recreational facilities (such as theaters, concert halls, and sports arenas), and more.

An architect can specialize in one of the above categories or take many types of assignments. Some architects are interested only in conserving and transforming old buildings for new uses, thus preserving our architectural heritage. The Italian architect Gae Aulenti won renown in the 1980s when she transformed the Beaux Arts Gare d'Orsay train station in Paris into the Musée d'Orsay for nineteenth-century French art. In 1997 she undertook the task of transforming San Francisco's old Main Library into new quarters for San Francisco's Asian Art Museum. Frederick Fisher of Los Angeles and David W. Prendergast of New York City spent three years renovating and expanding a huge Romanesque-Revival building, a former public school in Long Island City, New York. It opened in the fall of 1997 as one of the world's largest contemporary art facilities. Its name at that time, P. S. 1, fittingly described the building's origin. Today it is part of New York City's Museum of Modern Art.

Other architects concern themselves principally with urban or regional planning. Some go into related fields such as graphics, interior or industrial design, civil engineering, or construction management. Some even design structures for use in space in the future. Others work to integrate their constructions into the natural systems of the earth so they benefit all life, creating what is called sustainable design.

Some architects design not only homes but the furniture and accessories that go in them. The eminent architect Frank Lloyd Wright sometimes did this. Several of his houses with furnishings that he designed are now museums. The furnishings from a room in a Buffalo, New York, home he designed are displayed in the Metropolitan Museum in New York City in a replica of their original setting. The Finnish architect Eliel Saarinen, who designed the buildings for the Cranbrook Academy of Art in Bloomfield Hills, Michigan, and became the resident architect and director of the academy, designed a home and its furnishings for himself and his family at Cranbrook. It, too, is now a museum. Eliel Saarinen's son Eero, also an architect, said that his father seems to have seen architecture as encompassing everything from city planning to the designing of an ashtray for a table.

In the past the architectural profession was dominated by men, although in the first half of the twentieth century, Julia Morgan won acclaim for the more than seven hundred structures—both private homes and public buildings—that she designed. These were mostly in California. Now many young women choose architecture as their profession. In 1981 Maya Lin, a Chinese-American undergraduate architecture student at Yale University, won the commission to design the Vietnam Veterans Memorial in Washington, DC. She has since gone on to enjoy a successful career both as an architect and sculptor. The architect Elizabeth Plater-Zyberk was one of the founders of the Congress for the New Urbanism in 1993. This organization has drawn nationwide attention for advocating compact communities composed of neotraditional houses such as the community of Seaside, a resort town on Florida's Gulf Coast, which was designed by Plater-Zyberk and her husband, Andres Duany. In 2004 Zaha Hadid, an Iraqi-born British citizen, became the first woman to win the highest award in architecture, the Pritzker Prize.

The ability to conceptualize and understand spatial relationships is the most important requirement for anyone aspiring to become an architect. Artistic and drawing ability are helpful but not essential. Good communication skills, both oral and written; the ability to work independently or as part of a team; creativity; and computer literacy are also important. Increasingly computer ability is becoming a must. Computers are used for word processing, specifications writing, two- and three-dimensional drafting, and financial management, as well as an aid in designing.

## How to Get Started in Architecture

Anyone who aspires to become an architect should spend time in an architect's office, asking questions and watching what goes on. Many architecture schools offer summer programs for high school students. Attending one of these programs is a good way to get a sense of what architecture school is like and to find out whether you have the aptitude and stamina that is required.

After these experiences, if you still want to become an architect, you can secure the required training either by attending a university that offers a five-year professional architectural course or by obtaining a preprofessional undergraduate degree in architecture or a related area and then taking a two-year Master of Architecture program. Some schools offer a three- or four-year Master of Architecture program for students with a degree in another discipline. This last possibility is becoming the most common path.

After obtaining the required education, a would-be architect serves as an apprentice in the office of a registered architect, usually for one to three years, before being qualified to take the registration exam. The length of time that must be spent as an apprentice depends on the type of professional education the apprentice has had, which varies from state to state.

To find a position as an apprentice in an architectural office, you could ask your professors for advice as to how to proceed. Also, if you know an architect, you could ask her or him for advice. Either of these sources might be able to supply you with leads. You also could consult employment agencies about openings listed with them and scan the want ads in newspapers. Or, look in the Yellow Pages of telephone directories under the heading "Architects" and call or write letters to some or all of the firms listed, presenting your qualifications and inquiring if there is an opening for you.

Many architectural school graduates work in the field even though they are not licensed. A license is necessary only if you intend to work on your own. If you don't intend to work on your own, the only advantage of being licensed is that it gives employers a clear indication of your ability. To be licensed, you generally need to have earned a professional degree in architecture, have put in a period of practical training or internship (usually three years), and have passed the architectural registration exam of the state where you hope to work. If you want to work in the District of Columbia, you will have to take an exam there. A license allows you to build a structure only in that state, so many architects are licensed in several states. Once you are registered in one state, you can become licensed to build in other states simply by paying a fee to each state in which you wish to be permitted to work.

After you have served your apprenticeship and passed the state architectural registration exam, the firm you have been working for will probably continue to want your services. If not, or if you desire to work elsewhere, you could find a new position, go into business for yourself, or start a firm with friends. Some architects work for builders, real estate developers, or government agencies responsible for housing or community development, such as the Departments of Defense, Interior, Housing and Urban Development, or the General Services Administration.

In 2002 the median annual income for architects was $56,620. In the same year, the middle percent earned between $44,030 and $74,460. The lowest percent earned less than $36,280. The highest percent earned more than $92,350. Beginning architects who start their own firms may find that for a while their expenses are greater than their income, thus requiring substantial financial resources.

The time and effort involved in becoming an architect can bring great rewards, not only financially but also in personal fulfillment. The satisfaction an architect experiences when viewing a building he or she conceived and whose construction he or she guided to completion must be tremendous.

# 2

---

# BOOKBINDING

THE ART OF binding books by hand has changed little since the 1400s. Fine books bound by hand can be considered works of art on the outside as well as on the inside.

## History of Bookbinding

Bookbinding began in Greek and Roman times when books replaced scrolls. Authors wrote books on vellum, which is made from lamb-, kid-, or calfskin, or on papyrus made from the inner bark of the papyrus plant. Folded sheets of vellum could be stitched together, but papyrus is too brittle to be stitched, so holes were punched in the left edges of papyrus sheets and a cord run through the holes to keep the sheets in place.

At first, four folded sheets of vellum, called a *quire*, were used. Later, groups of quires were sewn to a strip of leather or vellum laid against the folds. We call these early books *codices* (singular form *codex*).

Early books were usually enclosed between two boards. Later their makers covered these boards with cured skins and, in time, decorated the leather covers, principally for church altars and royal patrons. Eventually the decoration became so elaborate that a book's cover might display the work of a jeweler, goldsmith, or ivory carver. Covers of precious metal inlaid with jewels, carved ivory, and enamel plaques survive, as well as leather covers similarly ornamented.

## What Bookbinders Do

The invention of the printing press brought about greater production of books, but the increase in quantity led to a decrease in quality. Today's hand bookbinders seek a return to excellence. They strive to emulate the high standards of their long-ago predecessors—not in the styles of the past, but according to modern ideas of good design.

Hand bookbinders lavish the time and care that goes into a hand-bound book only on texts they consider worthwhile from a literary standpoint. They also want the text to be attractively printed on paper of high quality. They sometimes discover desirable texts in used bookstores or secure them from rare-book dealers. Obviously the condition of the covers of the books they purchase doesn't matter since the covers will be replaced. However, such texts may need to be resewn. Hand bookbinders may bind texts newly printed by fine printers and texts of quality paperback books.

The inventiveness of bookbinders demonstrates how a book's cover serves as an artful and tantalizing introduction to the delights within. For example, for the cover of a Chaucer prayer book bought from a fine printer, Jeannie Sack impressed the outlines of a medieval village on beige leather. She onlaid pieces of beige leather over the doorways to accent them. She covered areas representing interior spaces glimpsed through doorways with brown leather to indicate the shadowy character of medieval interiors.

Eleanore Ramsey bound a book of Mother Goose verses with dark blue morocco. Bird shapes of silvery metal seemingly wing their way across the blue expanse.

Artists who bind books today sew the pages together in much the same way that Greek and Roman bookbinders sewed their texts long ago. If the pages come from a fine printer, one sheet of paper contains two pages (a folio), four pages (a quarto), or occasionally eight pages (an octavo)—the same system used by early bookbinders, who used vellum or papyrus sheets. The bookbinder folds the sheets so as to place the pages in proper order, then sews the folios, quartos, or octavos together, trims the folded edges, rounds the back, and glues a backing to it, perhaps adding padding for strength.

The bookbinder sews or glues narrow strips of cloth, called *headbands*, to the top and bottom of the back of the text. These headbands often display beautiful hand embroidery done with colored silk thread. Next the hand bookbinder puts stiff cardboard covers on the sides of the text, a step accomplished in many ways. One way is to lace the cords used to sew the pages together through the boards.

Hand bookbinders most often put leather over their cardboard covers and press lettering and designs into the leather by a process called *tooling*, leaving the impressions either unfilled or filling them with yellow gold, white gold, or palladium leaf. Silver is not used because it tarnishes. To get silver-colored tooling, either palladium or white gold or sometimes aluminum is used. As previously indicated, another way to make a design on leather is to inlay or onlay pieces of colored leather, metal, tempered glass, or any durable material.

Sometimes hand bookbinders use cotton, linen, silk, or other suitable cloth to cover the cardboards. If they decide on silk, they probably choose a velvet, damask, or satin weave, or they may choose a silk with metallic threads. The fabrics they use may be processed for stain resistance.

Hand bookbinders print lettering and designs on cloth by lithography, the silk-screen process, or tooling. Sometimes they paint or embroider designs directly on the cloth. (In the seventeenth century, English nuns and noblewomen embroidered exquisite book covers.) Beads incorporated in embroidery give a particularly sumptuous look.

Paper provides another kind of book cover, either over cardboard or, if sturdy, by itself. Another alternative is to cover the cardboard sides with paper and the spine with leather. Designs then can be printed or painted on paper in the same ways used on cloth. Bookbindings of papier-mâché offer another possibility. Persian artists in the seventeenth century painted papier-mâché bookbindings in jewel-like colors, portraying scenes of princely gardens or bucolic landscapes.

The bookbinder cuts the cover material large enough to fold around the edges of the boards. If the material is leather, the edges are pared to make them thinner so they will fold easily. The bookbinder pastes the leather to the boards, and to make the inner surfaces all the same thickness, he or she pastes paper the thickness of the leather edges to fill in the areas on the insides of the boards not covered by leather. Endpapers are then pasted in place.

One half of the endpaper is pasted to the inside of a cover while the other half becomes the first or last page of the book. Marbled papers or papers printed in a repeat pattern with a wood, metal, or linoleum block make attractive endpapers. Some endpapers have a scenic or other design printed or painted on them. A bookbinder either creates the endpapers or buys them from an artist who specializes in producing such papers.

To tool lettering or a design into leather, a hand bookbinder uses engraved metal stamps and tools that impress curved or straight lines. The bookbinder makes these stamps and tools or commissions someone else to make them. After assembling the necessary stamps and tools, the artist takes a strong, thin piece of paper and draws a design on it that the available stamps and tools can reproduce. The artist fastens the paper to the book cover with tape, heats the stamps and tools, and with them presses the lettering or design through the paper into the leather. The paper is then removed, the leather dampened slightly, and the pattern reworked with the stamps and tools heated just below the point where they would sizzle if tested with a few drops of water.

The artist may leave the tooled lines as they are (blind tooled) or inlay the lines with metal leaf. If the artist plans to inlay the lines with metal leaf, he or she paints the impressions with a solution called *glaire*, which acts as a binder. When the glaire dries, pieces of metal leaf are laid over the tooled lines. The stamps and tools are heated and the metal leaf pressed into the lines with them. After this, surplus leaf is wiped off. Tooling cloth covers requires a slightly different method.

To onlay a piece of leather or other material on a leather cover, one simply pastes it in place. To inlay, one cuts out an area of the cover the size of the inlay where the inlay is to go, then pastes in the inlay.

Sometimes a hand bookbinder gilds page edges, stains them with color, or paints or presses a design or scene on them.

Somewhere along the way, the bookbinder puts the book in a press. Different bookbinders do this step at different times. In fact, bookbinders use many different techniques throughout the whole process. The methods described here represent just a few of the methods used by hand bookbinders.

## How to Get Started in Bookbinding

Anyone who aspires to create artistic bookbindings needs to know the principles of design and how to draw, which can be learned in art school. After studying design and drawing, an aspiring bookbinder usually studies bookbinding with a teacher for several years. The art requires such precision that teaching oneself is almost impossible.

In the past, anyone wanting to learn hand bookbinding thought it necessary to study in Europe, particularly in France. This attitude no longer prevails, as one can study under excellent teachers in the United States.

One way to find a private teacher would be to go to an exhibition of fine bookbindings, such as museums or bookbinding guilds sometimes present, and then contact one of the bookbinders whose work was included in the exhibition and whose work you particularly liked. Or you could contact the special collections department of a university or public library for suggestions.

Upon request, the Guild of Book Workers will send you a booklet that lists its members—both schools and individuals—who teach fine bookbinding. The Guild can be reached at 521 Fifth Avenue, New York, New York 10175, http://palimpsest.stanford .edu/byorg/gbw. As not all schools that teach fine bookbinding are members of this organization, you could make inquiries of other schools to learn whether they teach this art.

Artists who wish to make a livelihood from fine bookbinding can contact fine printers, who are in a position to commission them to bind editions of books the printers have prepared. Or a bookbinder may do single bindings on his or her own and offer them for sale at exhibitions. Other fine bookbindings are made when an individual commissions a fine bookbinder to bind a book intended for a special presentation.

Not too long ago anyone who bound books by hand found it difficult to make a living in that pursuit. This situation no longer exists. Now many individuals take pleasure in owning books that are handsomely bound and are willing to pay high prices for them. Thus anyone who wishes to make a career of producing fine bookbindings can likely earn an income sufficient to support a satisfying lifestyle.

# 3

# CERAMICS

OBJECTS SHAPED FROM clay and then fired are called *ceramics*. A person who makes such objects is called a *ceramist*. Clay can be shaped into innumerable objects: plates, bowls, pitchers, cups, mugs, teapots, vases, trivets, tiles, plaques, sculptures, jewelry, lamp bases, and more. After shaping clay objects, the ceramist allows them to dry, fires them, usually in an oven called a kiln, and then perhaps decorates them in any one of countless ways.

## History of Making Ceramics

The ancient Greeks, Etruscans, Romans, Persians, Koreans, and Chinese particularly excelled in this art. The Chinese began making ceramics at least as far back as 2000 B.C. Even in the far distant past, they knew how to decorate their ceramics by carving designs into the clay, by applying pieces of clay for raised designs, and by painting designs on their wares. They also enhanced their ceramics with colorful glazes. Early on the Chinese also knew how to sculpt figures of clay, and they produced the first fine white ware now called porcelain, which we also call china because the Chinese invented it.

Pre-Columbian Indians of South America's west coast and Central America became accomplished ceramists in the distant past, as did the Indians of North America's Southwest later. Archaeologists believe the latter began making ceramics by covering baskets with clay and then letting them dry in the sun or placing them near cooking fires. Later, Southwest Indians placed their ceramics in open dung fires to bake, just as their descendants do today.

Around the end of the nineteenth century, a Hopi Indian found pieces of ancient ceramics at an archaeological site where he was employed. He brought them home to his wife, Nampeyo. Nampeyo studied the shapes, designs, and colors of the pieces and experimented making ceramics with the same materials her ancestors had used. In time she created ceramics that are valued highly. Thus an old art was revived.

## What Ceramists Do

Clay comes in a variety of colors—white, ivory, yellow, gray, red, blue, and black—and is found along the banks of streams and rivers, where water has deposited it.

Ceramists buy clay that is cleansed of pebbles and grit and mixed with other ingredients in the proper proportions to make earthenware, stoneware, or porcelain, the three kinds of clay bodies; or, they make mixes themselves. Ingredients mixed with clay that is to be used in making ceramics include ground stone (such as feldspar or flint) and/or sand. Sometimes a ceramist uses more than one kind of clay in a batch.

Earthenware is opaque, slightly porous, sometimes white, sometimes colored. Ordinarily it requires firing at a low temperature. Ceramists often apply glaze, which is a glassy coating, to earthenware; it can be either transparent, a colored-lead glaze, or an opaque tin glaze. Tin glaze contains lead as well as tin and is white or colored. The word *pottery* refers to earthenware.

Stoneware is nonporous and it is stronger than earthenware. Ceramists fire stoneware at a high temperature and traditionally in a smoky atmosphere. The colors of stoneware are usually warm and earthy. Chests of tea arriving in Europe from China in the seventeenth century introduced Europeans to stoneware, as each of these chests contained a red stoneware teapot. German, Dutch, and English ceramists quickly copied the material.

Porcelain, the aristocrat of ceramics, is white and when thin, translucent. It is the finest in texture of the three kinds of clay bodies. Like stoneware, porcelain is stronger than earthenware. When Chinese porcelain reached Europe in the Middle Ages, Europeans admired it and tried to duplicate it, but without success. Much to the frustration of would-be imitators, the Chinese refused to divulge how they made porcelain.

Finally, in the early eighteenth century, Johann Friedrich Bottger, a Berlin apothecary's apprentice, produced a true porcelain. Under the sponsorship of August the Strong, King of Poland and Elector of Saxony, Bottger set up a factory in Saxony (which is now part of Germany) for the making of porcelain. He used a white clay that is found in Saxony. This white clay is now called kaolin after the Chinese hills called Kao-ling, where the Chinese secured the white clay they used to make their porcelain. Mixing kaolin with ground feldspar and firing the mixture at an even higher temperature than that used for stoneware results in porcelain.

Bone china is porcelain containing bone ash secured by roasting and grinding cattle bones. Bone ash gives porcelain an ivory color and makes it less susceptible to chipping.

Before shaping a clay object, a ceramist kneads the clay, a process also called *wedging*. Kneading or wedging means working the clay with the hands until it becomes the same consistency throughout. After the kneading, the ceramist cuts through the clay repeatedly to eliminate air bubbles.

The most elementary way of making a clay container is to put a ball of clay in one hand, insert the thumb of the other hand into the center of the ball, and with the fingers of the latter hand rotate the ball. While the ball rotates, the thumb exerts pressure outward to increase the size of the center cavity. Simultaneously, the ceramist pinches the walls between thumb and fingers to make them an even thickness and to raise them to the desired height. The end result is called a *pinched pot*.

Many ceramists use the coiling method to make clay objects. Moist clay coils when placed in contact with each other adhere naturally. To make a clay pot by coiling, a ceramist holds a ball of clay in his or her hands and rolls it back and forth to form a snakelike piece of clay of uniform thickness. This roll of clay is then placed on a flat surface and coiled around and around itself until the coil reaches the size desired for the bottom of the planned object. The ceramist then smooths the clay. To make the sides of the piece, he or she coils a roll of clay on top of the outer edge of the bottom, this time working vertically and supporting the sides with the fingers to keep the sides from sagging, and at the same time uses the fingers to make the inner and outer surfaces smooth. For flared or inward tapering sides, one places the coils accordingly.

Another way of creating a clay object is the slab method. In this method, the ceramist flattens a ball of clay to an even thickness with a rolling pin, cuts pieces with the dimensions needed, and while the clay is still sticky, brushes the edges to be joined with slip, which is a mixture of clay and water that has the consistency of thick cream and that acts as an adhesive. The ceramist joins the edges to make the shape desired and fires the object. This method is used to make vases, tiles, sculptures, beads, earrings, or buttons.

Some ceramists make clay objects with a mold. In this method they either roll the clay to an even thickness and then press it into a mold, or they press moist clay into a mold without rolling it out first. Some consider using a mold a mechanical way of fashioning a clay object, but then creativity is called into play in the making of the mold.

Another way of making a clay object is with a potter's wheel, the prototype for which appeared at least four thousand years ago. A potter's wheel is a horizontal disc that revolves on a vertical spindle. In early times, a potter turned the wheel by hand, later by kicking the spindle, and still later by using a foot pedal. In the eighteenth century, someone introduced the idea of pressing a small boy into service to turn the wheel. Fortunately for small boys, electricity usually powers a potter's wheel today.

To use a potter's wheel, the ceramist places a ball of prepared clay in the center of the disc, dips his or her hands in water, and then clasps the clay with both hands. As the disc revolves, the ceramist presses the ball of clay inward. The pressure of the ceramist's hands causes the clay to rise. When the clay rises, the ceramist presses down the center with a thumb and repeats the process until the object becomes symmetrical and smooth, a condition that is called *centered.*

When the clay reaches this state, the ceramist again puts a thumb in the center and again presses down. Using the fingers of one hand in the center hole and those of the other to support the outside wall, the ceramist draws the clay outward until the base reaches the diameter desired. The centrifugal force of the revolving wheel helps move the clay outward.

To make the walls of the pot, the ceramist draws the clay upward to the height desired with the fingers of one hand inside the pot and the fingers of the other hand on the outside of the pot. For an outward swelling wall, the ceramist moves both hands outward while squeezing the clay between the fingers. For a wall curving inward, the ceramist collars the clay (makes a circle with the hands around the pot) so the diameter of the pot will not exceed the dimension desired. All the while, the ceramist keeps the surface of the wall smooth and the wall an even thickness. The spinning of the wheel assists in these endeavors and ensures symmetry.

Once a newly formed clay object has air-dried until it can be handled without losing its shape, a pattern can be pressed into the clay by the fingers or by using an object such as a comb, feather, sponge, wire, spatula, tool, or anything else that occurs to the artist as being suitable for his or her purpose. While pressing a pattern into clay, one hand supports the clay on the inner side.

When the clay has become medium stiff (leatherlike), a design can be incised into the clay with any blunt point, such as that of a lead pencil, a bobby pin fastened to a stick, the end of a knife blade, or a wire modeling tool purchased at an art supply store. Incising can be used to make either linear patterns or patterns made up of areas wider than lines.

A design also can be made by carving away what will be the background of the design; the elevated portion thus constitutes the design. Or one can cut all the way through the thickness of the clay body so that cutout areas comprise the design. Damp pieces of clay also can be applied to the clay body to make a type of design called *appliqué*.

A ceramist can give the surface of a clay body a coating of a different color by applying a colored slip to it after the object has become leather hard. If the clay used for the body fires to a white, cream, or buff tone, water can be added to some of the clay to make the slip and a metallic oxide added to the mixture to give color. Slips also can be purchased from an art supply store. The ceramist applies slip either by pouring, dipping, spraying, or using a brush. One can further decorate a slipped object by trailing a slip of another color over the base slip, say with a syringe; by painting a design with metallic oxides over the slip; by carving through the slip to make a design that exposes the color of the body; or by applying a colored glaze.

A ceramist can make glazes according to formulas or buy them ready-made. They can be glossy, matte, or semimatte. When applied to earthenware, glaze serves a practical purpose as well as a decorative one, as it makes earthenware waterproof. (Stoneware and porcelain are waterproof without a glaze.) Glazes can be colorless, serving as a sealer but not concealing the color of the clay body, or they may have color added to them. The color can be opalescent, semitransparent, or opaque. Glazes are applied in the same ways slip is applied.

In another method of decorating, the ceramist paints a design with wax on a clay object and then applies a coating of slip to the object. The slip doesn't adhere to the wax, so when the object is fired, the wax melts away. Because the slip adhered to the rest of the surface, the exposed original clay color that was covered with wax constitutes the design, while the body of the piece is the color of the slip.

The next step after the ceramist has decorated the object (if decoration is desired) is to fire the object in a kiln. A kiln can be any size and is usually heated by gas or electricity. Most often a kiln isn't heated until enough pots accumulate to fill it. The pots are carefully arranged on shelves in the kiln so that they will get the most benefit from the heat. Several hours or days may be required to get the kiln to the proper temperature, depending on its size. Once the proper temperature is reached, the kiln is allowed to cool for the same amount of time it took to reach the required temperature. After the proper amount of time has passed, the door of the kiln is opened and its contents removed.

Sometimes after a piece is thoroughly air-dried or after a first firing, a coating called an *engobe*, or underglaze, is applied. To make an engobe, one adds feldspar and silica to slip. These substances decrease the amount of shrinkage that occurs during firing, thus preventing cracking. A ceramist uses clays of different colors in making engobes and applies them in the same ways as slip is applied. When used under a transparent glaze, engobe colors appear brighter and truer than the colors of glazes. One can use a high or low temperature in firing engobes, but their bright colors fade as the temperature increases. Ceramists sometimes use engobes of other colors or metallic oxides to paint a design on an engobe coating. Using engobes to paint a design gives an artist more control than is possible when painting with glazes.

A clay object that receives further treatment after the first firing will require another firing after each addition of engobe to make it adhere permanently.

Clay has served as a medium for sculpture for thousands of years. Artists create clay sculptures by the coiling method or by forming the basic shape with large rolls of clay and pressing pellets of clay onto the basic shape to fill it out and add details.

Anyone who plans to make a large clay sculpture usually first experiments with clay on a small scale, then makes the object in the scale desired. A sizable clay sculpture needs an armature, which is an interior metal support made of either pipe or wire. The armature keeps the sculpture from collapsing before it is fired. When making a large sculpture, the sculptor stops work at intervals to allow the clay to dry somewhat; otherwise the object might collapse. During such intervals, the artist keeps the sculpture covered with a damp cloth to keep it moist enough so that clay added later will adhere.

When the sculpture is completely formed, the sculptor lets it air-dry until it is leather hard. Then the armature is removed and the piece fired.

Some present-day ceramists make jewelry. They shape clay into likenesses of flowers, leaves, vegetables, animals, geometric shapes, and other forms. They paint or glaze their creations, producing colorful and often whimsical necklaces, earrings, and pins.

The Arts and Crafts movement from 1895 to 1930 inspired ceramists of that era to create ceramics, both vases and tiles, that became an important component of the Arts and Crafts style. The tiles they produced were decorated with stylized designs, either in relief or incised, and given unusual finishes. These tiles were used for facades, interior walls, floors, stair risers, terraces, fireplace surrounds and hearths, friezes, and plaques.

These Arts and Crafts ceramists made their tiles by rolling out damp clay to flatten it, cutting the flattened clay into squares, and then pressing the squares into molds they had prepared. Their molds produced a variety of simplified, stylized designs: miniature landscapes, ships at sea, swans, children, and medieval motifs such as knights, maidens in flowing gowns, castles, and more. The squares were then dried, fired, and decorated with a variety of glazes.

Decorative ceramic tiles are still admired and can still be used in a variety of ways. Besides the uses they were put to during the Arts and Crafts movement, they can be used for murals, tabletops, framed wall hangings, picture frames, name plaques, house numbers, to decorate planters or birdhouses—anything one can think of. The interior walls of the St. Francis Sports Medicine Center in San Francisco are enlivened with life-size, individual figures engaged in various sports—a skier, a soccer player, a diver, a ballerina, a runner, and a tennis player—all made of flat, square tiles.

One ceramist found an unusual way of utilizing her skills. Clare Potter of Locust Valley, New York, fashions exquisite floral bouquets from clay. She fires her one-of-a-kind pieces once and then paints them with washes of water-based color. The resulting bisque finish (as opposed to a shiny glaze) makes her creations look natural. Her bouquets sell at high prices.

The high point in the creation of ceramics comes with the opening of the kiln after a firing, when the results of perhaps months of labor are revealed. Kei Fujiwara, a Japanese ceramist whose government designated him a National Treasure, still threw pots at age eighty. Almost every day he arose early and began throwing pots by seven o'clock. He fired his output but once a year, burning pine logs to heat his large kiln. The ash rising from the fire settled on the ceramics, creating artistic patterns. When at last the temperature in the kiln lowered sufficiently, Fujiwara, his family, and helpers gathered around the kiln. After the door of the kiln was opened, they gazed in awe at the beautiful creations of the master.

Art museums display ceramics made by artists of both the past and the present. Sometimes they mount special exhibitions solely of ceramics. Art galleries offer ceramics for sale. In the twentieth century the Spanish artists Pablo Picasso and Joan Miro and others raised the public's perception of ceramics from that of craft to an art form. Picasso's ceramics are as much admired as his paintings and sculptures.

In the United States Peter Voulkos, a professor of ceramics at the University of California in Berkeley, has opened new territories for artists and craftspeople everywhere. Voulkos has created a huge body of ceramic works, from vases and plates to large sculptures such as the Gallas Rock, an eight-foot-high abstract figure that stands in the sculpture garden of the University of California at Los Angeles. From 1955 to 1960 he created five thousand unique pieces. His classes and workshops have inspired experimentation and stylistic diversity with the result that his former students are recognized as leading ceramists of the day.

## Using Your Ceramics-Making Skills

You could become part of a growing trend by opening a shop where customers decorate bisqueware with designs of their own creation to take home with them after it has been fired. The owner of such a shop forms and fires the bisqueware in advance of offering it for customers' use. The owner of the shop or an assistant is always present to give any necessary instruction. Customers get a great deal of satisfaction out of the creative process and perhaps come back on future occasions to decorate more pottery.

Some ceramists, of course, teach. Teaching positions are available not only in schools but also in such places as community centers, senior centers, YMCAs, and YWCAs.

As objects made of clay are useful and/or decorative, the demand for them will surely always exist. Perhaps this is the field where you should direct your artistic talents.

# 4

## DRAWING

ONE OF THE first things students in art schools learn is how to draw, as drawing is fundamental to almost all other visual arts. For example, painting is drawing on canvas, paper, wood, ceramic, or whatever; engraving is drawing on metal; etching involves drawing on a wax ground covering metal; lithography involves drawing on a stone or other hard surface; and making a wood-block print involves drawing on wood. Also, drawing ranks as an important art in its own right and proves an asset in many vocations.

## History of Drawing

Drawing must surely be the oldest of the arts. Among the first evidences of the appearance of humankind on our planet are images drawn or incised on cave walls and ceilings and on other rock surfaces. Perhaps before the creation of images such as these, our ancestors drew in the mud or dust with sticks.

During antiquity and the Middle Ages, drawing developed along with the other arts. Monks and nuns embellished manuscripts with intricate drawings enhanced with color. Artists who produced mosaics and murals undoubtedly drew preliminary sketches. Builders of Gothic cathedrals surely made drawings of the facades and interiors they planned, as did stoneworkers of the sculptures required for the cathedral's adornment.

## What Drawers Do

The equipment required for drawing is minimal: something to draw with, something to draw on, and for drawing outdoors, a folding stool for sitting on and a drawing board to support the material on which to draw.

Long before the graphite pencil came into existence, artists used charcoal for drawing. Charcoal remains a popular drawing medium today. Both graphite pencils and charcoal can make lines of varying width, and the broadside of a piece of charcoal can cover wide areas. Because charcoal doesn't adhere as closely to a drawing surface as graphite, rubbing charcoal lines with a finger or cloth creates a shaded area. Spraying a charcoal drawing with a fixative prevents smudging.

Chalks and crayons of any color are also used for drawing. They are most effective on coarse-grained, tinted paper. In times past, artists preferred red and black chalks. Today most artists who use chalks prefer pastel colors. The resultant works are called pastels. Chalk drawings smudge easily. Applying a fixative to a chalk drawing destroys its unique quality, so chalk drawings are best kept under glass.

Ink also serves as a drawing medium. Many artists prefer India ink, which is a deep black. If desired, they thin India ink to secure shades of gray. Some artists use colored inks for drawing, or watercolors, tempera, acrylics, or oil paints. With these latter fluids, the question of whether a work is a drawing or a painting remains a moot point.

Artists use various instruments to transfer liquid to the drawing surface. Today stores stock a wide variety of pens for drawing with ink. Felt pens and brushes offer another possibility for transferring a fluid to paper. Ancient Chinese drew with a brush and ink, and many modern artists prefer this method. Brushes give greater variety of stroke width and tone intensity than other drawing instruments. Also brush strokes result in less clearly defined edges than those obtained with other instruments—a desirable quality in some instances.

These days drawing is also done with computers. Art schools are teaching their students how to draw with the aid of a computer. When drawing with a computer, one can move components around to find the best arrangement.

Paper ranks as the preferred surface for drawing—colored paper as well as white. A pale cream, a light gray, or light brown makes an attractive background. One can give white paper a pale wash of watercolor to get a desired tone for the background. With a colored background, a drawing medium in a dark tone proves the best choice.

Other materials used as a drawing surface include cloth, wood, metal, vellum, ceramic, glass, even a wall. With some of these materials, indentations made by the drawing tool give a third dimension.

Once equipped, anyone wanting to make a drawing faces the question of what to draw: landscape, still life, figure composition, portrait, nature study, fantasy, or abstract or nonobjective drawing.

If landscape is chosen as the subject, some teachers suggest making a finder, which is a frame cut from cardboard proportionally the same shape as the finished work is to be. Looking through the finder held at arm's length with one eye closed and moving the finder around helps in deciding what portion of a landscape will make a good subject. An artist includes in a drawing only those elements of the landscape he or she sees that will make for a good composition. If desired, one can shift the elements around in the sketch or make additions from one's imagination, or a landscape can be completely imaginary.

If the artist decides to use components of a real location for a landscape drawing, he or she first sits so that the glare of the sun doesn't fall on the paper and then perhaps makes small preliminary sketches to try out different compositions. From these he or she selects one to develop fully. Some artists make this decision from mental pictures without the aid of sketches.

Most often the basic ingredient of a drawing is line: thick, thin, any width in between, straight, curved, jagged, wavy, or an accented line—one that starts out strong then diminishes until it fades away, leaving its continuation to the imagination of the viewer. Parallel lines drawn close together (called *hatching*) or two sets of parallel lines that cross each other (crosshatching) indicate shadows or other dark tones. Dots can serve the same purposes as lines. A few artists use only dots in their drawings.

When making a drawing, one does not need to fill all the space on whatever is being used as the ground. Empty space can serve as important a function as lines and/or dots. Empty space can represent many things: the sky, a stretch of earth, water, the planes of a face, the smooth areas of a garment, the surface of any object.

David Hockney, one of the most popular contemporary artists, says that anyone can be taught to draw well. He points out that drawing makes one look more carefully, for drawing requires intense observation, thereby increasing one's perception of the world. People who take up drawing observe things they otherwise would fail to notice. In short, drawing can enrich one's life.

Drawing can serve as an aid to thinking, a way of evolving ideas. Sculptors and ceramists sometimes make drawings to help them decide the form they want their art to take. Weavers draw patterns to serve as guides. Fashion designers, industrial designers, interior designers, architects, and landscape architects all draw to develop their ideas and also use their drawings to explain their ideas to employers, employees, clients, and prospective clients. Drawings can often convey many ideas more explicitly than words. Today with the increased use of computers for drawing, artists are exploring what are called moving drawings that incorporate what happens over time as well as what happens in space to more accurately convey our experiences.

## Using Your Drawing Skills

Knowing how to draw can lead to a career as an illustrator for books, magazines, newspapers, and advertisements of all kinds. Some illustrators win immortality, as Beatrix Potter did with her charming drawings and tales of Peter Rabbit. And can anyone who has read Wanda Gág's *Millions of Cats* forget her drawings of cats, or Maurice Sendak's drawings of fearsome creatures in *Where the Wild Things Are*? Though these illustrators wrote the stories that accompany their drawings, the artwork in most publications is done by someone other than the authors. If you are interested in being an illustrator for children's books, you may want to look at the book *Children's Writer's and Illustrator's Market*, edited by Alice Pope and published by Writer's Digest Books, P.O. Box 420235, Palm Coast, Florida 32142; www.writersdigest.com.

Some individuals skilled in drawing use their talent as cartoonists. A successful cartoonist develops a distinctive and appealing style. Sometimes the style involves caricature, that is, it emphasizes certain features of an individual. Political and editorial cartoons comment on current events and attempt to sway public opinion, and they often succeed. In the nineteenth century, the political cartoons of Thomas Nast exposed the corruption of a notorious political machine headed by one Boss Tweed that was bilking both New York City and the state of New York out of millions of dollars. Nast's cartoons helped bring about the downfall of Tweed and his henchmen. Nast also originated the elephant and donkey symbols of the Republican and Democratic political parties and introduced the modern depictions of Santa Claus.

Cartoons that aim to amuse utilize either a single picture with a short gag line or a series of pictures with spoken words in balloons. In the latter case we call them comic strips. *New Yorker* magazine featured Peter Arno's single-picture cartoons lampooning New York City café society and the idle rich over a period of many years. A heavy, bold line characterized Arno's style, while Edward Koren, whose cartoons began eliciting chuckles from the readers of *New Yorker* magazine somewhat later, uses thin, squiggly lines to cover the bodies of his curious characters who stand like humans, talk like humans, and find themselves in humanlike situations, but whose heads and furry bodies resemble members of the animal kingdom. Publishers issue collections of the work of some cartoonists in book form, and museums and galleries sometimes exhibit the drawings of cartoonists. An exhibition of Koren's drawings was shown in museums in several cities some years ago.

If drawing comic books interests you, Darren Auck, art director of Marvel Comic Books, advises, "Draw constantly. Be original. Stress storytelling. Comics are more than pin-up pages with word balloons." Marvel offers internships and drawing tests for aspiring artists. Salaries for artists who produce comic books range from about $100 a page for pencil work to much more.

Animated cartoons offer another outlet for people skilled in drawing. Walt Disney pioneered this field. Through animated cartoons he gave the world Mickey Mouse and scores of other delightful characters. He and the company he founded also have brought beloved folktales to life in movies with the aid of drawings as well as original stories. Drawn characters even interact with real actors in some movies.

The California Institute of the Arts, familiarly known as Cal Arts, is a highly respected training ground for animators. It was founded by Walt Disney and is located in Valencia, California, a suburb north of Los Angeles. Its rivals include Sheridan College near Toronto, Canada; the Ringling School of Art and Design in Sarasota, Florida; the School of Visual Arts in New York City; the Pratt Institute, also in New York City; and the Academy of Arts College in San Francisco.

Animators secure employment not only with movie and TV studios, but also with companies that produce video games. The former director of Cal Arts' experimental animation program, the late Jules Engel, used to travel to studios to appeal for jobs for his students. Now representatives from the studios contact Cal Arts seeking to hire students. Many artists and animators work in this genre. Web design is another opportunity open to them. Some animators move into writing, directing, and producing. A few even become millionaires. Walt Disney, for instance, never drew anything except at the beginning of his career.

The median annual income of salaried multimedia artists and animators was $43,980 in 2002. The middle 50 percent earned between $33,970 and $61,120. The lowest 10 percent earned less than $25,830, and the highest 10 percent earned more than $85,160.

An interesting career open to people who draw is that of a medical illustrator. A medical illustrator must have not only artistic ability but also a detailed knowledge of living organisms, surgical and medical procedures, and human and sometimes animal anatomy. A bachelor's degree combining art and premedical courses is usually required, followed by a master's degree in medical illustration, a degree offered by a few accredited schools in the United States.

Scientific and technical illustration is another field open to those who can draw and who have a suitable background.

People with drawing talent may choose to go into fashion illustration—that is, drawing illustrations of women's, men's, and children's clothing and accessories for newspapers, magazines, catalogs, and other types of media. A fashion illustrator might work for an organization that manufactures clothing and accessories or for a retail outlet.

If a person with drawing skills is proficient at catching a good likeness of a person, he or she could choose to become a portraitist, working either in oils, pastels, ink, or charcoal.

Another endeavor in which a person can use drawing skills had its beginning hundreds of years ago in Italy. At that time, artists drew images of the Madonna and other religious subjects on the ground in front of Catholic churches. Onlookers would throw coins upon the drawings to show their appreciation. Some businesses are now beginning to use a descendant of this activity—now called street painting—as an advertising tool. An artist creating a street painting with colored chalk on a sidewalk or plaza is sure to draw crowds, as people are fascinated by the process. Realizing this, businesses hire artists to create street paintings as a way of promoting sales, shopping centers, and festivals; the opening of new restaurants; and the like. The subject of a street painting doesn't have to be concerned with the event taking place nearby; it can be anything that is eye-catching. Advertising agencies are always looking for new ways of promoting their clients' interests. Some advertising agencies have featured artists doing street painting in TV ads for advertisers such as 7 UP and Bank of America. You could contact an advertising agency in your town and interest those in charge in having you create street paintings for some of its clients.

Some galleries, among them the Drawing Center in the SoHo district of New York City, show only drawings. The director of the center, Ann Philbin, believes showing drawings by new artists to be the center's most important mission. She says drawings appeal particularly to young collectors, because drawings are often more affordable than, say, paintings.

Drawings can fetch high prices. In the fall of 1995, a drawing, *Self-Portrait with Raised Elbow* by Egon Schiele, sold at Christie's auction house in New York City for $1.87 million. If you hope to make your living by selling your drawings, it probably would be necessary to supplement your income by teaching or with some other job until the day comes when your drawings are in sufficient demand to make other employment unnecessary.

In any event, if you love to draw, undertaking a career that involves drawing may be the path you should take.

# 5

# FASHION DESIGN

FASHION DESIGNERS DESIGN clothing for women, men, teenagers, and children. They design accessories such as hats, shoes, handbags, and belts. They also apply their talents to designing furniture, silverware, glassware, china, sheets, car interiors, and any product where styles change.

In spite of all these possibilities, one usually thinks of a fashion designer as someone who designs clothing for women. No doubt this state of mind prevails because more people are interested in women's fashions than in any other fashion area. The media focuses considerable attention on women's fashions, compounding the interest, but today men's and children's fashions are increasingly in the news.

## History of Fashion Design

Attention to personal adornment is certainly nothing new. Fashion documents go back as far as the Stone Age. Cave and rock paintings, incised images, and carved stone figures from that era show both men and women wearing items that go beyond what would be necessary for protection or modesty. Carved stone female figures, found in Central Europe and that date from twenty-four thousand to thirty-two thousand years ago, sometimes wear bracelets, beads, an apron, or a waistband. Sometimes what appear to be tattoos or painted decorations adorn their bodies. It is apparent that all over the world, even as far back as prehistoric times, people used clothing, jewelry, tattooing, and body paint to enhance their appearance.

The mid-nineteenth century saw the introduction of the sewing machine, followed by the invention of paper patterns. Previously fashion as a commercial venture catered only to the wealthy, but as a result of these advances, fashion for the masses became possible. Illustrated magazines devoted to women's fashions appeared, and a new awareness of dress swept Europe and America. Paris ruled as the undisputed center of fashion, and Charles Frederick Worth, though an Englishman, reigned as the leader of the Parisian couturiers. In his establishment on the Rue de la Paix, he designed clothes that expressed his artistic talent. Women from Europe and America clamored for his creations.

By the 1930s, American fashion editors and buyers crisscrossed the Atlantic by ocean liner to attend the seasonal openings of Parisian couturiers. They quickly noted every new trend and cabled word back to their publications or employers. Manufacturers and the fashion-conscious public eagerly awaited their pronouncements. Fashion editors and buyers still go to Paris openings, but these days they fly and also go to openings in Milan, New York, and elsewhere, as Paris is no longer the unchallenged center of fashion.

Nowadays, many American fashion designers receive as much acclaim as their European counterparts. Most of them work in New York City, where the garment district around Seventh Avenue serves as the center of the industry. Other American fashion designers center their operations in Los Angeles, San Francisco, Dallas, or Atlanta. Sometimes clothing carries the designer's name. Other times the designer remains anonymous; instead of the designer's name, the garment carries the name of the manufacturer.

## What Fashion Designers Do

Fashion designers get started in many ways. Perhaps their mothers or grandmothers taught them to sew. Maybe they studied art in high school, college, or art school or attended an institution devoted exclusively to fashion, such as the Fashion Institute of Technology in New York City or a similar school elsewhere. Incipient designers sometimes begin by making clothes for themselves and their friends; then they sell a few models to stores or open their own boutiques. In time some designers own their own fashion houses or perhaps even their own factories.

Other aspiring fashion designers get into fashion design by circuitous routes. They may begin in the retail business, become buyers, and then branch out into designing. Some begin as window display designers or work in textile studios. Some begin as milliners, interior designers, even furniture designers. Others start by designing for the ballet, theater, movies, or television. (Edith Head, until her death the preeminent clothes designer for the movies, began as a sketch artist. Her first sketch that became reality was a costume for an elephant in a Cecil B. De Mille extravaganza!)

A few designers study architecture and decide to design clothes instead of buildings. The approach in both professions is somewhat the same; both architects and fashion designers strive to create functional structures with good proportions and allover good looks. Both may use a drawing board to develop their ideas. Today both are relying more and more on computers to visualize their creations.

The idea is the essential element that the designer supplies. After getting an idea, the designer may make a sketch illustrating the idea. Some designers start their careers by selling their ideas to manufacturers or by sketching fashion illustrations for newspapers and magazines. Other designers may use computers to develop custom-designed clothing for a wider public than possible when tailor-made clothing was done by hand. Known as made-on-demand (MOD) or mass customized clothing, made-to-order fashions are part of the decentralization of production made possible by the digital revolution. A few companies that sell exclusively over the Internet use a made-to-measure artificial-intelligence computer program that can create a personalized pattern for every customer's body.

Other fashion designers arrive at their ideas by draping fabric on a model. A female designer may drape a fabric on herself or on a mannequin, live or otherwise, to see how the material falls. Cutting and sewing follow. From this master sample, a pattern is made.

Some designers haunt museums in the hope of picking up ideas. Paintings, prints, and sculptures sometimes show fashions of other days, and some museums exhibit clothing from other eras and other cultures—Oriental, Russian, Gypsy, Eskimo, Indian (either Eastern or Western), the Tyrol, Tibetan, or whatever. Some designers travel the world in search of stimuli.

In recent years fashions from other eras or decades—the days of the old West, the Victorian period, the flapper era, the fifties, the sixties, and the seventies—all reappeared in new guises. Time and time again never-out-of-style classics come to the fore with new twists.

Some fashion designers display a fascination with the ultramodern and ponder what the future will bring. Even the space program affects fashion. André Courreges, for one, admires the purity of aerodynamics as demonstrated by the airplane and spaceship. He reflects this admiration in the clothes he designs—simple, functional garments suggestive of the life we may live in the future. Designers who favor the ultramodern look often use materials such as vinyl, Plexiglas, or surplus electronic parts. Designers told Lucille Khornak, when she interviewed them for her book *Fashion 2001*, that the future may bring temperature-controlled clothing, disposable paper fashions, and spray-on, peel-off bodysuits.

Contemporary modes in other arts also influence clothing design. For instance, styles in interior design and architecture are sometimes echoed in clothing design, as are movements in painting and sculpture—movements such as cubism, futurism, surrealism, op art, and pop art. The colors used by a popular painter, say David Hocking, reappear in wearing apparel. Anyone familiar with the work of the Dutch painter Piet Mondrian has undoubtedly seen clothing that has geometric designs and colors reminiscent of his paintings.

Fashion designers even keep a lookout for new trends that appear on the streets—trends usually started by young people. There are even companies that do trend research and sell their findings to clothing designers. These companies hire scouts to cruise the streets to discover the latest fads. These scouts use video to record their findings.

For the most part, however, fashions evolve. The ideas of one year's collections usually derive from those of the preceding year. Rarely does a drastic change burst on the scene. Following World War II, one such drastic change did occur—Christian Dior's "new look." During the war, authorities froze fashion along utilitarian lines. By the time restrictions were lifted, women were ready for something different. Dior gave them that something different—an ultrafeminine look with shaped bosoms, cinched waists, and multiple petticoats under billowing skirts whose hemlines reached mid-calf. (During the war, a government decree had kept hemlines at midknee.) The drastic change caused a sensation. Since that time, hemlines have fluctuated all the way up to miniskirt length, down to ankle length, and to most every length in between.

In the early years of the twentieth century, a fashionable woman changed clothes several times a day. She wore one outfit in the morning, another for going out to lunch. In the late afternoon, she slipped into a tea gown or cocktail dress. In the evening, she donned a dinner dress, a theater dress, or sometimes a ball gown. Today woman are too busy to make so many changes.

Today a piece of clothing must be appropriate for many occasions. It must reflect the times we live in. It must move easily, be comfortable, and be easy to care for. Like generations of women before them, today's women want choices that allow them to present to the world an image of what they are or what they aspire to be. Women want their clothes to flatter them. Designers try to meet these requirements. For the most part, designers save their romantic notions for gowns for important evening occasions.

Designers seek materials that are the best available or affordable. Some designers travel abroad, say to France or Italy, looking for beautiful fabrics. They may order fabrics made to their specifications, hand-dye fabrics themselves, or even manufacture their own cloth. Some designers silkscreen, print, or paint designs on fabric, or add appliqué or trapunto, which is a type of raised embroidery. And all the time they keep their eyes on current trends or maybe start some, as Norma Kamali did when she used sweat-suit material for thirty-five different kinds of clothing, from miniskirts to harem pants.

To qualify as a work of art, an article of clothing must appeal through the combination of its shape, line, color, and texture, plus perhaps an element of surprise. The Metropolitan Museum of Art in New York City has an extensive fashion collection.

The makers and devotees of one type of clothing confidently call the clothing they produce wearable art, implying that clothing designed by other types of designers fails to qualify as art. Clothing referred to as wearable art is usually a one-of-a-kind creation—say a combination of stripes, large florals, little prints, and tapes. Perhaps its maker knitted it, crocheted it, or had it handwoven in many colors with three-dimensional effects, or embellished it with painting, drawing, embroidery, quilting, beading, lush velvets, ribbons, bits of lace, strips of fur, or any of a myriad other items. Such clothing often resembles a fantasy conjured by a genie. Clearly designers of so-called wearable art hope to rid the world of drabness. Other designers ingeniously recycle materials to create sought-after apparel that is also earth friendly, or they promote old clothing such as used Levis as the latest fashion.

According to U.S. government data, the median annual income for fashion designers was $51,290 in 2002. The middle 50 percent earned between $35,550 and $75,970. The lowest 10 percent earned less than $25,350. The highest 10 percent earned more than $105,280.

Anyone who chooses fashion design as a career enters a world that can be exciting and glamorous as well as financially rewarding.

# 6

---

# FINE PRINTING

PRINTERS OF FINE books are passionately concerned with the appearance of the books they produce and aspire to publish only texts with literary merit. To this end they carefully consider not only the contents of a text but also the quality of the paper they use, the type they choose, the layout of each page, the artwork, and the overall design of each volume.

## History of Printing

In the Middle Ages European monks and nuns created beautiful books. They copied the texts in magnificent script on vellum and filled vacant spaces with geometric designs and miniature plant and animal forms. They further decorated their books by embellishing the capital letters with color and gold. Museums and other collectors now value these early manuscripts.

Books that we would consider works of art gradually ceased to be made in the Western world after Europeans learned to print. The

Chinese learned to print over a thousand years ago, but knowledge of this development didn't reach Europe until after Europeans learned to print on their own, some five hundred years ago. Printing, of course, was not feasible without paper. The Chinese first made paper in 105 A.D., but over a thousand years passed before the art of papermaking spread to Europe. The Crusaders brought this knowledge home with them when they returned from their wanderings.

At first, early printers tried to ornament their books in the way monks and nuns decorated manuscripts. This effort lasted but a short while. As more people learned to read, the demand for books grew. As printers worked to meet this demand, they gave less and less thought to the appearance of their output.

A turnabout came in the late nineteenth century when proponents of the Arts and Crafts movement in England protested against machine-made products. They deplored mass-produced articles as lacking the beauty of objects made by hand. As a result people became more appreciative of handcrafted items, manufacturers gave more attention to the design and quality of their products, and fine printing won recognition as a worthwhile endeavor. Through the years a few dedicated individuals devoted themselves to producing books of high quality. In recent years this trend has accelerated.

Formerly printers of fine books concentrated on the classics, such as the works of Shakespeare and Walt Whitman. Today they also give their attention to contemporary poetry and prose. The prose chosen by fine printers for their books includes biography, journals, essays, and fiction. Today's fine printers also produce art and photography books and sometimes posters and other items.

Because of the amount of labor involved in the making of fine books, and because the market for them remains relatively small due to the high prices necessarily charged, fine books come on the market only in limited editions, usually consisting of no more than five hundred volumes. The value of books from fine printers usually increases with time, for as time goes by, they are probably no longer available from the printer, and people with discriminating taste prize them.

## What Fine Printers Do

A fine printer uses paper of the highest quality. Such paper comes from England, France, Italy, or one of the small paper mills in the United States that make superior papers. Rag pulp is the principal ingredient of such papers. The makers of quality paper use molds to produce one sheet at a time.

Some fine printers come close to ecstasy over the beauty of a handmade paper. Modern commercial publishers mostly use paper made from wood pulp. Paper made from wood pulp disintegrates in fewer than fifty years. Consequently, books made by fine printers will prove the only books of our time capable of surviving through centuries.

A fine printer buys type from a foundry, as well as small pieces of metal to separate words. The type and the pieces to separate words are made of lead and sold in fonts. A font includes letters of the alphabet, figures, and punctuation marks, all in the same size and style. A variety of styles and sizes is available. A fine printer chooses well-designed styles appropriate for the texts. In addition to buying type from a foundry, a fine printer keeps on the lookout for old ornamental initials cut into wood or engraved on zinc. Some fine printers design chapter initials themselves and create plates to print them.

Fine printers often choose line drawings for the illustrations in the books they print. They print these line drawings from zinc engravings, collographs, etchings, woodcuts, or linoleum cuts. A fine printer either prepares the plates to reproduce the line draw-ings or commissions someone else to do so. Some printers hand-paint illustrations.

A fine printer often incorporates innovative features in a book, such as making a volume wider than usual, taller and narrower than usual, or using pages of an unusual shape. Foldouts, accordion-pleated pages, or covers of an unorthodox material such as Plexiglas may be used. Sometimes thin wooden sheets or other unexpected materials serve as slipcases. Out-of-the-ordinary touches can add to the appeal of a book.

Fine printers today use essentially the same methods their pre-decessors used in the early days of printing when type was set by hand, letter by letter, with a tool called a *composing stick*. Today's fine printers employ this method particularly for special pages, such as the title page, that require more consideration of design than do other pages. Sometimes a fine printer has the type set by machine. A monotype machine sets each letter individually, while a linotype machine casts an entire line at a time.

The printer locks the type for pages printed at the same time and any illustrations intended for those pages into a metal frame. If the printer wants the illustrations in another color of ink or in more than one additional color, each color used will require a separate operation.

Usually fine printers use a small press powered by a treadle or motor. The press's rollers ink the type. Then a platen, a flat metal plate, presses the paper against the inked surface, transferring a reverse image of the metal type and illustrations onto the paper. This process, letterpress printing, was the traditional way of print-ing before the introduction of offset printing, the method now used by most commercial printing firms.

The next steps involve folding the printed sheets and gathering them so that the pages come in the right order, sewing the pages together, and then trimming and binding them. A fine printer performs these operations or allots them to a bindery.

A fine printer makes the cover for the book or delegates both the binding and the making of the cover to an artist who specializes in bookbinding. Making the cover involves designing, printing, cutting, and gluing as well as careful consideration of proportions, color, lettering, and decorative elements, so that the cover harmonizes with the appearance of the printed pages.

Leather is usually considered the most desirable material for bindings, though the high cost of leather sometimes prohibits its use. An artist considers making a binding of leather an exciting opportunity. Even covers of cardboard covered with cloth or with a cloth spine and paper-covered sides are expensive. Of necessity, a fine printer usually covers most of an edition with paper wrappers.

Anyone who decides to become a printer of fine books embarks on an exciting and probably lifelong love affair with beautiful books.

# 7

# GLASSMAKING

GLASS HAS MANY functional uses; one can scarcely imagine getting along without it. But glass is also prized as an ornamental object when it is formed, colored, and/or embellished in unique and beautiful ways.

## History of Glassmaking

Glassmaking apparently began in the Near East, perhaps as long ago as 4000 B.C. Someone discovered that a combination of silica and alkali melted by intense heat and then allowed to cool results in the glittering substance we call glass. To improve the quality of the glass, other substances are now added to the basic mix of silica and alkali.

The oldest known glass objects are glass beads, amulets, and vases found in the tombs of Egyptian pharaohs. The beads date back to somewhere soon after 2500 B.C. By the eighteenth dynasty (circa 1480 B.C.), Egyptians were shaping glass vessels around a core of clay and decorating them with threads of glass in contrasting colors. They also made glass objects by pressing molten glass into molds. They set colored opaque glass in gold and used it in combination with precious and semiprecious stones to create exquisite necklaces, bracelets, and rings.

The most important innovation in the history of glassmaking was the invention of glassblowing. Someone around the time of the birth of Christ, perhaps in Syria, blew a glob of molten glass on the end of a hollow tube into a mold. The next step came with the realization that one could shape a molten glass glob on the end of a tube by blowing it until it reached the desired size and then working it with various tools, all the while revolving it to prevent it from collapsing. Adding handles and feet when wanted and decorating the glass in various ways followed.

After these discoveries, the glass industry underwent extensive expansion. Glassmakers became so skillful that modern practitioners of the art sometimes face frustration if they try to duplicate treasures handed down from the past.

## What Glass Artists Do

To make clear glass, a glassmaker mixes chemicals called *fluxes* with sand and an alkali. Fluxes help the batch fuse. Manganese or lead serves as a flux and at the same time decolorizes the mix. After combining the ingredients, the glassmaker heats the mixture in a crucible in a gas furnace that has been heated to say 2,500 or 2,700 degrees Fahrenheit. When the mixture has melted, the heat is turned down and the glass mixture allowed to cool to 1,800 degrees.

To do glassblowing the artist then takes a glob of molten glass (called a *gather*) on the end of a long metal blowpipe (called a *pontil*), pulls the blowpipe from the furnace, shuts the furnace door, and blows into the blowpipe, thereby creating a bubble that adheres to the end of the pipe. When the bubble reaches the desired size, the glassmaker coaxes it into the desired shape with tools, all the while twirling it to counteract the pull of gravity. Occasionally the glassmaker puts the glass bubble, still on the end of the blowpipe, into a reheating furnace called the *glory hole*. A few moments in the glory hole keeps the glass soft enough to continue working it.

When the glassblower is finished shaping the glass, it is removed from the blowpipe and put in an oven with a temperature of about 1,000 degrees Fahrenheit. The temperature of the oven is then allowed to decrease slowly, usually overnight but perhaps for several days if the object is large. This process of heating and cooling is called *annealing*. Annealing makes the glass stay intact; otherwise it would shatter. In this way an artist can create a beautiful object from a molten mass derived from ordinary materials—pure magic!

To make a mold-blown object, an artist also begins by taking a glob of molten glass on the end of a blowpipe. The artist then blows into the blowpipe to make a bubble of molten glass of the required size, lowers the bubble into the mold, and closes the mold tightly around the neck of the blowpipe at the point of attachment. The artist blows into the blowpipe until the glass expands enough to fit the mold, and then rotates the assemblage until the object solidifies. The number of rotations necessary depends on the size of the object and how fast it cools. When it is deemed that the object has cooled, the object is removed from the mold and put in the annealing oven.

After the object is removed from the annealing oven, rough edges on the bottom of the object where it was attached to the blowpipe can be removed by chipping, grinding, or polishing.

Some glass objects are not given any embellishment, but if desired, they can be decorated in many ways: by adding color to the glass mixture after the annealing, by painting a design on the glass with enamel, or by cutting, engraving, etching, or sandblasting a design into the glass.

Glass can be given color by adding a metallic oxide to the mix. Today's glass artists turn out multicolored vases, bowls, bottles, carafes, plates, and goblets using a wide range of colors: chartreuse, ivory, celadon, aqua, lavender, opaline white, and candy pink as well as classic colors such as amethyst, topaz, turquoise, cobalt, and ruby. An object can be entirely of colored glass, or decorations of colored glass can be added to a clear glass object. To add colored decorations, an assistant takes a blob of molten colored glass on the end of a metal rod called a *punty*. The assistant brings the colored blob in contact with the glass object at a designated point. The glassmaker then revolves or otherwise moves the object so that colored glass is drawn out onto the object where wanted, manipulates threads of colored glass with a comblike tool called a *pick* to make a pattern of parallel lines, or dips into or dabs the object with colored molten glass or cold glass chips.

Rolling the object in a metal cup after colored glass has been added or pressing it with a block of wood will make the colored additions flush with the surface of the glass object and expel any trapped air. This latter action can result in layers of swirling colors much like the colors in some abstract expressionist paintings.

Once the artist is satisfied with the result, he or she puts the piece back in the glory hole for a brief period so the additions will fuse with the body.

Painting on glass with enamel has a long history. Magnificent enameled glass lamps hung in Egyptian mosques as long as six hundred years ago, a Quranic metaphor for God's light. By the late fifteenth century, Venetian glassmakers were enameling and gilding glass goblets and plates. In the seventeenth century, artists in Germany painted scenes and coats of arms with enamel on large drinking cups called *beakers*. Museums exhibit examples of different types of enameled glass.

To decorate a glass object with enamel, an artist can cover an area of the glass with enamel, put the object in a warm kiln for a short time to partially dry the enamel, and then use a pointed instrument to scratch off some of the enamel to make a design. This method is called *sgraffito*.

In an alternate method, when the surface is more or less flat and clear, the artist tapes a paper with a design on it to the underside of the glass as a guide. If the glass is not transparent, the artist can transfer the design to the upper glass surface with tracing paper. The artist then paints the design on the glass with enamel. With either of these methods, the last step is to fire the glass in a kiln at a high temperature so as to fuse the enamel to the glass. The glass is allowed to cool before removing it from the kiln.

The art of decorating glass by cutting a design into it goes back at least to Roman times. The Romans no doubt were inspired to cut designs into glass as a result of their having carved rock crystal to produce handsome objects, for rock crystal when polished has the look of fine glass. Ancient cut glass thought to be from Egypt, Persia, and Byzantium still exists.

Lead glass is the most lustrous glass and is also comparatively soft, so it is the most desirable for cutting. George Ravenscroft of England first produced it about 1675. Lead glass is made by adding lead oxide to the glass mix. When held in sunlight, cut lead glass sparkles as if hidden fires burn in its depths. It is used to make handsome tableware and decorative pieces. Faceted pendants made from lead glass appear jewel-like.

To make a cut-glass object, the artist first draws the design on a glass object with, say, a felt pen or India ink. The drawn lines serve as a guide for cutting. If the design is intricate, only the major lines may be drawn. In that case the artist cuts finer lines without the aid of guidelines.

Glass is cut with glass cutters by holding the glass against a revolving iron or steel wheel with a container above it that dribbles fine damp sand onto the area being cut. Later the cuts are smoothed and polished by using a wooden wheel and rouge and putty powder, then a paste of pumice with a cork, felt, or leather wheel. Or the cut can be smoothed and polished by dipping the object in acid. The latter method does not give as desirable results as the former, traditional method.

In the eighteenth century a glass tax levied in England led to the closing of glassworks there. Two Irish brothers, George and William Penrose, recruited unemployed English glassworkers and established a glassworks at Waterford, Ireland. Cut glass from Waterford is famous to this day. Glass cutters at the firm of Baccarat in France, founded in the nineteenth century, also have created distinguished cut glass, as have American glass cutters, particularly in the late nineteenth century and early twentieth century. These artists sometimes combined cutting and engraving on the same object.

Engraved designs also are cut, but the cuts are not as deep as designs that are referred to as cut glass. In the traditional way of engraving glass, small copper wheels grind away glass to form a pattern. The wheels are aided by an abrasive combined with oil. Artists also can engrave on glass by using a pencil-shaped tool with a diamond point to make designs of lines, dots, or a combination of the two. Or, glass can be engraved with an electric vibrating engraver or with an electric drill. A vibrating engraver has a Carborundum or diamond point that makes small white frosted dots and lines.

The practice of engraving on glass goes back several centuries. Bohemia, now part of the Czech Republic, was first noted for engraved glass in the seventeenth century. Bohemia's Emperor Rudolf II so admired the work of the country's first glass engraver, Kaspar Lehman, that he gave him a title of nobility. Through succeeding centuries portraits, scenes, mottoes, coats of arms, emblems to commemorate important events, and purely decorative designs have been engraved on glass in many countries.

Flashed glass is glass that has a layer of colored glass covering a layer of clear glass or glass of another color. An electric drill can be used to grind away areas of the outer layer of glass to form a design that reveals the underlying layer.

Designs are etched into glass in one of two ways: In one method an acid-resistant substance is applied to the parts of the glass that are not to be etched. In the other method the whole piece is covered with the acid-resistant substance and the design is scratched in. In either case the next step is to dip the glass into hydrofluoric acid, which eats away the exposed glass, forming the design.

Designs engraved or etched into glass are usually not polished, though they may be. An unpolished surface has a rough, frosted look; polished surfaces, of course, are smooth and clear.

Sandblasting designs into glass gives the artist greater control than does etching and avoids the noxious fumes of the acid method. To sandblast a design into glass, the artist covers the object with a mask that has a cutout design. With compressed air, the artist blows sand against the exposed areas, thereby sculpting the design. Artists who sandblast designs on glass are sometimes commissioned to create panels for architectural settings in high-fashion restaurants and major hotels. Artists also sandblast designs on smaller glass objects.

Other ways of working with glass include casting, sculpting, allowing glass to slump before hardening (usually into a mold), constructing sculptures from commercially available glass and new adhesives, and fusing sheets of differently colored glass. The makers of *millefiori* (Italian for "a thousand flowers") paperweights fuse colored glass canes to achieve their effects. Other artists enclose or embed in glass whatever strikes their fancy: concrete, wood, mesh, wire, plant parts, or enamel. Sometimes an artist allows a cloud of bubbles to remain in glass for its decorative effect. The ways of creating art with glass seem endless.

One of today's preeminent glass artists is Dale Chihuly, who was a student of Harvey Littleton, the ceramics professor who with scientist Dominick Labino developed formulas for glass whose mix melts at a low enough temperature to permit artists to have glass furnaces in their studios.

Chihuly's imagination has led him to produce many different kinds of glass objects. One example is the *Glass Forest*, which he developed with his associate James Carpenter. *Glass Forest* is a veritable jungle of abstract glass trees and vines filled with argon and neon gases.

Chihuly's interest in Indian blankets and baskets led him to make nonfunctional glass vessels reminiscent of these artifacts. To make these vessels, he weaves colored glass rods that are in a malleable state, making both thick-walled cylinders and thin-walled "baskets." Rolling a red-hot cylinder over the woven rods fuses them and sometimes pleasingly distorts the object. Sometimes after allowing his "baskets" to slump in varying degrees, he nestles them within one another.

Chihuly also makes vases and sculptures with ruffled edges, biomorphic forms, and variegated colorings that are suggestive of tropical shells and flowers. Even chandeliers are in his repertoire.

Chihuly is perhaps the greatest living glass artist. He is one of only three American artists to have been given a solo show at the Louvre Museum in Paris. His work also has been exhibited at the Seattle Art Museum and at the American Craft Museum in New York City. In 1992 he was named the United States' first National Living Treasure.

The Pilchuck Glass School, which Chihuly cofounded fifty miles north of Seattle in the Cascade mountains, offers a summer program. Glassblowing, engraving on glass, stained-glass techniques, and other ways of creating art with glass are taught.

With ingenuity a glass artist can build an engrossing career and perhaps become another superstar in the art world.

# 8

# GRAPHIC DESIGN

THE ESSENCE OF graphic design is to express an idea in a visually noticeable form. That is the goal of today's graphic designers, one that remains unchanged from that of its predecessors.

## History of Graphic Design

The term *graphic design* first came into use in the 1920s to describe the art of visual, eye-catching communication. Actually the concept of eye-catching communication goes back to ancient times. The Sumerian scribes who invented writing by devising cuneiform characters and pressing them into clay tablets were graphic designers. So were the Egyptian scribes who combined words and images on rolls of papyrus. The Chinese artists who invented wood-block printing were graphic designers. So were the monks and nuns of the Middle Ages who laboriously copied texts in elegant script and decorated their pages of vellum with geometric designs and miniature plant and animal forms.

Throughout the centuries more ways of visual communication have evolved: metal-type printing, engraving, etching, lithography, serigraphy, photography, television, computer graphics, and many others.

## What Graphic Designers Do

Traditionally graphic designers' tools have been pens, pencils, scissors, print, and film media. Today graphic artists usually use computers to create art that meets their clients' needs. With computers they can lay out and test various designs, formats, and colors before printing a final design.

Graphic artists create designs for advertisements, books, magazines, newspapers, brochures, posters, catalogs, billboards, exhibitions, packaging, labels, signs, corporate logos, letterheads, TV commercials, audiovisual presentations, point-of-purchase displays, and almost anything in the design field their clients may request. Some clients want a graphic designer to design the total image their company presents to the world—not only the logo, the letterhead, brochures, annual reports, and such, but the look of the company's buildings, anything that can help make a favorable impression on the public. Such clients recognize design as a major way of developing a favorable reputation.

Not only must a graphic designer produce the required material, he or she must be able to work effectively with other people. Usually a beginning graphic designer works under an art director. In addition he or she must deal with numerous other people: copywriters, editors, account executives, promotion managers, and researchers. Also a graphic designer must be reliable and willing to work overtime if a job demands it, and, of course, a graphic designer's output must please the client.

# Using Your Graphic Design Skills

An obvious area for a graphic designer to work in is advertising. Advertising agencies produce printed advertisements and material for broadcast on radio or TV or for projection as audiovisual presentations. They may also design annual reports for corporations. Once those in charge, in conjunction with the client, decide upon a campaign, the design department begins work on the project.

The first step is to analyze the requirements and gather all relevant information. For printed material the designer makes small sketches, called thumbnails or layouts, that indicate possible placement of print and illustrations in the finished piece. From these experiments, the designer chooses the best one and develops it into a full-size so-called comprehensive (often called a *comp*)—first a tentative "rough comp" suggesting what the finished product will look like, then after incorporating any desired changes, a "tight comp" that more closely resembles the finished product. It shows blocks of print (often set in type) and includes copies of photographs or other kinds of illustrations enlarged or reduced to the proper size, if necessary, by a photostat machine. The individual in charge presents the finished comprehensive to the client for acceptance or rejection.

For film and video presentations, the design department prepares material on storyboards. Storyboards show a series of images with accompanying dialogue printed below the images. Audiovisual presentations developed from such storyboards may involve any combination of multiple projectors, multiple screens, narration, music, and sound effects. Advertising firms develop such productions for corporations to show at conferences or exhibitions or to customers or potential customers.

Computers can aid graphic designers in preparing charts, graphs, illustrations, and animated sequences. With a pen or mouse, the graphic designer draws on the electronic tablet or mouse pad. Color can be added with the aid of computer systems designed for that purpose. Two systems that allow the designer to add color are Pantone and CMYK. When using one of these systems, the designer can designate the color wanted in any given area. The process of converting electronic art into a printed piece, however, is a complicated one and not for the uninitiated.

A graphic designer who loves books finds working for a book publisher particularly rewarding. The duties of a graphic designer working for a book publisher include determining the number of typewritten characters in a manuscript by a method called copy fitting, selecting the typeface, securing the illustrations, and planning the position of the printing and illustrations on the pages by using grids. With this material the graphic artist makes a layout, or dummy, and then a pasteup (also called a mechanical) that shows the placement of all elements that will make up the book. The graphic designer creates the cover design for a book and decides upon the type of binding. Good choices in these matters result in an attractive, well-organized book.

A graphic designer who works for a magazine publisher proceeds in much the same way as a designer who works for a book publisher. The basic design of the covers of all issues of a magazine are usually the same with only printed matter and illustrations changed. The presentation of articles, however, varies.

Packaging involves three-dimensional planning. The artist develops layouts and comps for the sides of a package in the same manner as for other printed material. Relaying the required information in the most appealing fashion remains the ultimate goal.

Once only the province of architects, industrial designers, and display manufacturers, exhibition design now also falls within the scope of the graphic designer. Exhibition design requires two-dimensional and three-dimensional planning. The designer devises the floor plan and prepares signs and displays that perhaps use not only type but also photographs, movies, video, animation, and audiovisual presentations.

A graphic designer draws inspiration from all the visual arts, past and present, and from cultures all over the world. The inspiration may come from, say, Oriental art, cubism, surrealism, art nouveau, art deco, op art, pop art, or any of innumerable possibilities, but no matter where the initial inspiration comes from, a graphic designer develops his or her own style—or many styles.

## How to Get Started in Graphic Design

Anyone wanting to work in the field of graphic design can acquire the necessary skills by getting a bachelor's degree in fine art, graphic art, or visual communication. Studies leading to such a degree will preferably include a basic course that serves as an introduction to graphic design, explains design theory, and discusses the concepts of visual communication. Schools offering such studies also offer training in skills such as drawing, painting, photography, typography (the art of designing with type), and perhaps calligraphy. Other courses cover advertising design, publication design, corporate design, packaging design, and point-of-purchase design. In addition the graphic-design student learns color theory, production techniques, and the use of film, video media, and storyboards—panels that depict successive scenes for a television commercial or other video presentation. A good graphic-design course also requires students to take liberal arts courses, as a wide base of knowledge and interests increases one's chances of success.

Before seeking employment, a would-be graphic designer should prepare a portfolio of projects he or she has designed in school or as a freelancer while in school or after graduation. The individual will then have concrete evidence of his or her skills to show to a prospective employer. Or it may be that upon graduation, an individual entering the graphic design field prefers to work as a freelancer, developing a clientele of his or her own.

In 2002 the median annual income for graphic designers was $36,680. The middle 50 percent earned between $28,140 and $48,820. The lowest 10 percent earned less than $21,860 and the highest 10 percent earned more than $64,160.

Graphic designers make significant contributions to our culture. They help convey information effectively and compellingly, thus aiding the economic well-being of the world. They also give us pleasure visually, thereby counteracting dullness and adding a certain zest to life.

# 9

# INTERIOR DESIGN

THE PROFESSION OF interior design evolved from the profession of interior decorating. Interior designers see their role as broader than that of the traditional interior decorator. The latter mostly suggested color schemes and offered choices of draperies, slipcovers, furniture, and carpets. Interior designers concern themselves with these matters, but they also are concerned with the organization of space. They may develop designs and prepare working drawings and specifications for new interiors as well as interior changes in existing buildings and then oversee the subsequent construction. Such changes may include the removal of walls, the widening of doorways, and the installation of new bathrooms, kitchens, windows, lighting fixtures, fireplaces, moldings, and finishes. Interior designers also may be concerned with the addition of wings. Increasingly they use computers to devise layouts and develop designs. When layouts are on a computer, they can be easily changed to comply with the desires of the client.

## History of Interior Design

Several centuries ago the only buildings whose interiors were furnished and embellished with the idea of creating beauty were cathedrals and palaces. Then in the eighteenth century, English cabinetmakers such as Thomas Chippendale and Robert Adam (who was also an architect), in addition to designing furniture (and in the case of Adam, buildings) for their wealthy clients, also designed curtains, carpets, ceilings, and moldings for them. As late as the nineteenth century, both in England and the United States, the homes of ordinary people for the most part contained only a few pieces of furniture. These pieces of furniture were chosen on the basis of their functional performance, with little thought given to aesthetics or beauty.

Recognition of interior decoration as a profession began around the beginning of the twentieth century. Edith Wharton in her manifesto *The Decoration of Houses* is usually credited with upgrading interior decoration into an art. In the early nineteen hundreds, Elsie de Wolfe, later Lady Mendl, espoused the idea in the United States of beautiful and comfortable homes. She emphasized uncluttered rooms with flowered, glazed-chintz slipcovers and a mixture of furniture from different periods. She was the first to create modern kitchens with laborsaving appliances. At Wanamaker's in New York City, Ruby Ross Wood established the first decorating department in a department store. In London, Syrie Maugham became well known for her all-white rooms.

After World War II, magazines such as *House Beautiful* came into being and promoted the idea of attractive living quarters for almost everyone. These magazines made it known that professional decorators were available to help in making desirable choices. Interior decoration grew into an enormous business. In the 1950s and

1960s the profession of interior decorating widened its scope to that of interior design.

## What Interior Designers Do

Interior designers concern themselves with the interiors of houses, apartments, hotels, motels, restaurants, stores, showrooms, offices, banks, churches, museums, passenger ships, corporate jets—any place where functional, aesthetic, and/or image-promoting surroundings are desired. Some interior designers not only design interiors for their clients but also the furniture to go in them. Sometimes they design exclusively for firms that manufacture furniture, fabrics, wallpaper, carpets, lighting fixtures, glassware, chinaware, flatware, or other items used in interiors.

An interior designer's professional status is attested to by membership in The American Society of Interior Design or The National Society of Interior Designers. Both of these organizations require their members to have college-level training, five years' experience, and a sound business record.

Some interior designers do not prepare for their careers by formal study. Some start as apprentices to established designers; some begin their careers as architects or come to the profession by other routes. Designer Ward Bennett went from fashion sketching and window display to interior design when an apartment he decorated for a family connection was admired by others who then requested his services. Sarah Tomerlin Lee took over her husband's design business when he died. Before that, she had edited *House Beautiful* magazine and worked as an advertising executive. She soon became a preeminent designer of hotels and inns.

The essential requirement in interior design is creativity. An interior designer visualizes what changes or additions to a structure might be desirable or necessary, concocts interesting color schemes, senses what will go well together, and arranges the contents of rooms in ways users find aesthetically pleasing as well as functional.

An interior designer knows about period furnishings and design, about the kinds of paint and their suitability to different kinds of jobs, and judges the quality of wallpaper, fabrics, furniture, accessories, and carpets and other floor coverings such as tile, vinyl, linoleum, cork, and more. He or she knows about possible window treatments and how to measure for draperies and slipcovers. To plan structural changes, an interior designer understands building techniques and knows about building materials and their sources and where to find expert craftspeople.

An interior designer keeps on hand samples of different types of materials to show to clients: paint chips, fabric samples, floor covering samples, tiles, window blind samples, and so on. He or she also collects manufacturers' catalogs picturing furniture, plumbing fixtures, hardware, and anything else for which a client might have a need.

An interior designer learns the client's needs and then seeks out items to fulfill those needs. Though he or she may visit many manufacturers' showrooms in search of the right items, only a few alternatives, or perhaps only one, are presented to the client for a particular need.

Early in the relationship, the designer and the client decide on a budget and the method of payment, and then they sign a contract. The design departments of home-goods stores usually make no charge for services rendered. They make their profit through the purchases contracted for by the client. Other interior designers get their remuneration by charging a client the retail price for purchases, for which the interior designer pays the wholesale price. Still other interior designers charge a flat fee or a percentage of the costs.

An interior designer can either work for himself or herself, for an interior design firm, or for a department store.

In 2002 the median annual income of interior designers was $39,180. The middle 50 percent earned between $29,070 and $53,060. The lowest 10 percent earned less than $21,240, and the highest 10 percent earned more than $69,640.

Nowadays most interior designers seek to create environments that make for pleasant living rather than trying to adhere to hard-and-fast rules. The rules of decorating have never been more relaxed. Seemingly incongruous pairings are acceptable if they contribute to a composition that makes an impact. Manhattan designers Kevin Roberts and Timothy Haynes believe that a Louis XVI settee and a skateboarding teenager can coexist in the same living room. What they work for is an atmosphere of easy elegance. They let the dynamics of life decide where the furniture should go.

# 10

---

# JEWELRY MAKING

JEWELRY MAKING IS a highly skilled and ancient art. From earliest times, people have been attracted to jewelry because of its beauty and because they can use it to express their own artistic natures.

## History of Jewelry Making

In primitive times people used materials close at hand to make jewelry. Other than teeth and bones, they used shells, pebbles, feathers, tusks, and wood. Later amber, washed up on shores and also found in the ground, and lignite, a brownish coal also from the ground, provided additional material. Still later, people discovered gold and semiprecious and precious stones deposited by water on the banks of streams and rivers. Oysters yielded pearls, and in time people recognized silver as a material suitable for jewelry. When the ancients discovered how to make glass, they used it in conjunction with gold and precious and semiprecious stones to make jewelry.

Ceramic beads also date from remote times, as does the art of enameling.

Unfortunately, through the centuries jewelers took apart much of the jewelry made by their predecessors, so as to be able to reuse the stones and metals. Consequently not much jewelry from the past survives.

Most of the early jewelry still in existence has been found in tombs and caches buried at times of invasions. Jewelry from the fourteenth century B.C., found in the tomb of the Egyptian boy king Tutankhamen, comprises the largest collection of jewelry and objects of gold in the world. The quality of the workmanship is superb and unsurpassed by modern jewelers. The tomb of Puabi, a Sumerian queen of the third millennium B.C., also revealed a hoard of fabulous jewelry. This cache included every type of jewelry known today: pins, rings, necklaces, wrist and arm bracelets, pectorals, diadems, and huge gold earrings. The makers of these items knew almost every technique used by modern jewelers.

Early in the twentieth century, rumor held that a grand duke of Russia gave Coco Chanel, the French fashion designer, a collection of jewelry, which dazzled beholders with diamonds, rubies, emeralds, and pearls. Coco commissioned jewelers to make copies of her jewelry, and then sold the copies to her customers. In these copies, paste "jewels" substituted for real gems. Paste jewels are made of glass and cut in the manner of real jewels. The history of paste jewels goes back to medieval times and earlier. In some periods their value exceeded that of real stones. The term *costume jewelry* refers to such fake concoctions.

In the 1960s, Jay Kenneth Lane made fashionable the use of plastic "stones." He used them first in the chandelier earrings popular at that time. Chandelier earrings dangled a couple inches or more from the earlobes and oftentimes fairly dripped with jewels, making them heavy and consequently painful to wear. Substituting plastic for the real thing solved the problem. Lane went on to use plastics in other pieces of jewelry with dramatic effect. Even those who owned authentic jewels clamored for the so-called junk jewelry.

Today's jewelry designers sometimes mix fake stones with real gems. They let their imaginations run free. They use almost any material—including iron, steel, brass, and fiber—in their creations. We still have a higher regard, however, for precious and semi-precious gems and metals than for substitutes.

## What Jewelry Makers Do

The first step in creating a piece of jewelry is to decide upon a design. Inspiration may come from nature, from man-made objects, by doodling on paper, or out of the blue. Styles in other arts may be an influence; some jewelry reflects the tenets of cubism, futurism, art deco, or abstract art. Artists also get inspiration from jewelry of other periods. Paintings, sculptures, ceramics, and mosaics from the past sometimes show the kinds of jewelry worn in other times.

The artist may refine an idea by sketching on paper or constructing a prototype from heavy paper, cardboard, metal foil, wire, clay, wax, string, or pliable scrap metal. He or she probably experiments with ideas, combinations, and proportions before executing the final form.

An artist who wishes to create metal jewelry learns a variety of techniques. One such technique is annealing, which means heating metal and then letting it cool. Metal thus treated becomes softer and so easier to work. Another technique a jeweler uses is fusing metals by the use of heat and soldering. Hammering or reticulation gives metal an attractive texture. Reticulation is a process that causes a silver alloy surface to wrinkle. Blackening portions of a metal surface with sulfur compounds enhances a design and intensifies the color of a stone. Heating metal and then dropping it into an acid solution for a few minutes, a process called *pickling*, cleans the metal.

An artist may cut metal for jewelry from sheet metal and shape it with hammers or pliers, or he or she may pierce sheet metal to make openwork designs. Appliqué involves cutting forms from sheet metal and soldering them to another metal surface.

Wire also is suitable for appliqué or openwork designs. A jeweler bends the wire with fingers or pliers to make wavy or curving lines or figures comparable to line drawings. Wire twisted by a special machine creates an interplay of light and shadow. Wire also is used to support pendants. Filigree refers to designs made of very fine wire.

Granulation is a technique whereby a jeweler attaches granules of metal, especially gold, to a base of the same metal to form silhouettes or other patterns. Many ancient cultures used granulation to make exquisite jewelry, but in later centuries no one understood how the ancients had been able to fasten tiny grains of metal securely and neatly to a metal base. In the twentieth century experimenters finally discovered ways of duplicating the granulation of the past. Whether the granulation processes used today are the same as those of ancient times no one knows.

To make cast-metal jewelry, a jeweler models the desired form in wax and covers it with a heat-resistant plaster or similar material. The assemblage is then heated. The wax melts and runs out through channels provided in the plaster, thus creating a mold. The jeweler pours molten metal into the mold, allows the metal to harden, then removes the plaster. Voila! A metal image of the wax model stands revealed. In centrifugal casting, the mold, filled with molten metal, is spun to make certain the metal reaches all extremities. Centrifugal casting makes possible the rendering of intricate details.

One of the oldest techniques used to put a design on metal is chasing, which makes a linear design. The artist first draws the design on the metal with a tool called a *tracer*, then uses a hammer and tools called *punches* to indent the metal along the lines indicated by the design. The artist usually makes the punches for a work at hand to ensure that their shapes fill the requirements of the job. Hammering the punches against the metal where it is to be indented causes the metal to stretch in those areas, thus forming the design wanted. Hammering done from the back is called *repoussé*, a French word meaning "to thrust back."

Engraving is another ancient technique that jewelers use to make a design on metal. Engraving is done by cutting the surface of the metal with a sharp tool. The incised design looks similar to a line drawing.

Artists also etch designs into metal. In this technique, the artist covers the metal with etching ground, which may be wax or a tar-like substance. When the etching ground dries, the artist cuts a design into the etching ground with needles and other tool, thereby exposing the metal. The artist then immerses the metal in an acid bath. Etching ground is acid-resistant, so the acid etches only the exposed metal. The artist removes the metal from the acid bath after the acid etches the metal to the depth desired for the finest lines. The artist then covers these lines with a stop-out varnish and returns the metal to the acid bath. The stop-out varnish prevents the acid from acting further on the lines it covers. When other lines reach the depth desired for them, the artist applies stop-out varnish to them and returns the metal to the acid bath. The artist repeats this process (called *biting*) as many times as desired. After the completion of this process, the artist removes the etching ground with a solvent. The artist scratches the design through the resist to expose the metal underneath.

The final steps in making metal jewelry are filing (if necessary to remove irregularities), cleaning, polishing, and buffing.

Diamonds, rubies, emeralds, and sapphires are the stones considered precious. Chrysoberyl, topaz, and transparent zircon are sometimes added to this list. The semiprecious stones are amethyst, garnet, aquamarine, amber, jade, turquoise, opal, lapis lazuli, and malachite. The animal products pearl and coral also count as gems. Supply houses furnish jewelers with both cut and uncut stones. In many localities a beach, banks of streams, or other rocky areas yield attractive stones.

When making traditional jewelry, a jeweler usually cuts a stone in one of two ways: in convex form, in which case it is polished and called a *cabochon*; or faceted, which means it is cut with many small planes that reflect the light. Makers of nontraditional jewelry use stones of any shape, left as they are or tumble-polished in a special device. A drill can be used on stones to produce openwork, an incised design, or a design in relief.

Cut stones are usually held in place by prongs or set in a bezel, a metal rim encircling the lower part of a stone. Faceted stones look best when held by prongs, as the elevation prongs provide allows light to pass under the stone, adding to the sparkle. Artists usually use a bezel with a cabochon or step-cut stone, though sometimes they use prongs for these. Cradles of wire can be used to hold uncut and tumbled stones.

Some artists use opaque or transparent enamel in jewelry making. Enamel is made from powdered glass colored with metal oxides and diluted with water and an adhesive. When the mixture is heated, it melts. As it cools, it crystallizes and adheres to sur-

Your specialty could be using beads to make jewelry. Some towns have shops that sell beads and everything needed to create jewelry from beads. Such shops carry beads of glass, wood, metal, enameled metal, ceramic, semiprecious stones, abalone, bone, horn, porcelain, plastic, and more. In planning a piece of jewelry, one can line up the beads one is planning to use in the channels of a bead board—a plastic tray covered with flocking to keep the beads from rolling. By doing this you can see how the finished piece will look and make whatever changes desired before threading the beads.

If your town doesn't have a shop that sells jewelry-making supplies, you could order them from the catalogs of companies that specialize in selling jewelry-making supplies. Two such sources are Fire Mountain Gems, www.firemountaingems.com, and Rings & Things, www.rings-things.com.

## How to Get Started in Jewelry Making

*The Book of Beads*, by Janet Coles and Robert Budwig, gives detailed instructions for making jewelry from beads, as well as design ideas. It also lists resources for beads and beading supplies. Some shops that sell beads and beading supplies offer classes in jewelry making.

Barron's publication *Profiles of American Colleges* lists colleges and universities that offer a major in jewelry making under the heading "Metal/Jewelry." Some technical schools and local colleges also offer courses in jewelry making. Attending classes in jewelry making is the best way to learn this skill. Also, having had formal training improves one's employment and advancement opportunities. Courses in technical schools and local colleges vary in length from six months to three years. These courses teach their students

rounding metal. An enamel area is best built up in three o
layers. After the addition of each layer, the artist heats the pie
a kiln and then allows it to cool. After the final layer cools, po
ing completes the process. Polishing makes the enamel more
trous and intensifies the color.

The three principal types of enameling that artists incorpoi
into jewelry are cloisonné, champlevé, and plique-à-jour.

In the cloisonné method the artist makes a design with thin go
silver, brass, or copper strips placed on edge on a sheet-metal ba
covered with enamel. The artist fills the enclosures made by th
strips with enamel of various colors. After the heating and coolin
of the final layer of enamel, the artist grinds the surface of the
enamel so the upper edges of the metal strips show. The word *cloisonné* comes from a French word meaning "to partition."

In the champlevé method the artist fills depressions in a metal
surface with enamel. *Champlevé* is also a French word meaning
"raised field."

Plique-à-jour enameling allows one to look through transparent
enameling and so gives the effect of stained glass. The artist pierces
a design through a piece of metal or makes a design with wires, filling the empty spaces with transparent enamel. Plique-à-jour enameling shows off to best advantage in jewelry through which light
can flow—objects such as earrings or ornamental hair combs. Th
word *plique-à-jour* means "light of day" in French.

Jewelry may be made by shaping clay into miniature likeness
of flowers, leaves, vegetables, animals, geometric shapes, or an
thing else desired. After shaping these components, the cerami
fires them, paints or glazes them, and then combines them to pr
duce colorful and often whimsical necklaces, earrings, bracele
and pins.

the use and care of jewelry tools and machines and give instruction in design, casting, stone setting and polishing, and repairing. Jewelry-making skills also can be learned through correspondence courses that last several years.

Some technical schools and correspondence schools offer programs that give training in appraising and others that lead to a gemologist diploma. Such courses generally last about six months. On the other hand, correspondence courses that include instruction on how to identify and evaluate diamonds and colored stones, as well as on appraising, gemology, and designing jewelry, can last several years.

Even though one has had formal training, three or more years of on-the-job training is desirable so as to be able to refine one's skills and learn about the operation of a shop.

Some people learn jewelry making by serving as apprentices to established jewelers, or they teach themselves. Arthur King, an outstanding American jeweler, taught himself while overseeing an empty navy troopship. He practiced on bits of scrap metal. Many leading jewelers taught themselves. Books can aid those who wish to follow their example.

New York City ranks as the jewelry center of the United States. The displays of jewelry in shops on and off Fifth Avenue in that city equal those of the finest shops anywhere in the world. Also hundreds of small jewelry manufacturers, dealers, and retailers line Forty-Seventh Street in New York City. Many of these enterprises boast their own designers, who sometimes become officers of the companies for which they work.

According to the U.S. government, in 2002 the median annual income for jewelers and precious stone and metal workers was $26,260. The middle 50 percent earned between $19,500 and

$35,310. The lowest 10 percent earned less than $15,030, and the highest 10 percent earned more than $45,620.

Potential buyers of jewelry can be found almost everywhere, so no matter where his or her base of operations may be, an artist who makes good-looking jewelry is almost certain to find an appreciative clientele.

# 11

# LANDSCAPE DESIGN

INDIVIDUALS, DEVELOPERS, CORPORATIONS, and governmental agencies engage landscape designers to create pleasurable open spaces— areas such as parks, private gardens, roof gardens, private estates, plazas, playgrounds, and the grounds of shopping centers and new towns. Landscape designers also design plantings for indoor spaces if a client wants to bring a bit of nature inside, say under a glass roof. They oversee the work involved in bringing their designs into being and devise plans for their maintenance. They also formulate management programs for forest and wilderness areas.

## History of Landscape Design

Landscape design began when primitive people first rearranged the environment outside their shelters to make it more to their liking. As long ago as 2800 B.C. the villas of well-to-do Egyptians included gardens replete with tree-lined avenues, ponds for waterfowl, and pavilions in which to laze away idle hours. The ancient Greeks enjoyed atriums, the rectangular patios around which they built their houses. The Romans cultivated small town-gardens and at their country estates, large garden complexes. Extensive ruins of the gardens of the Emperor Hadrian's villa near Rome attest to the Roman love of vast parklike spaces.

The vogue for formal gardens spread to France, where the landscape designer André Le Nôtre planned the gardens of Versailles outside Paris for the Sun King, Louis XIV. Others of the European nobility copied Le Nôtre's concepts on their estates.

By the eighteenth century, English country gentlemen began to view the subjection of nature as seen at Versailles and its imitators as too artificial. Under the tutelage of landscape designer Lancelot "Capability" Brown, they sought a return to more natural surroundings. At the same time philosophers extolled the virtues of the "noble savage," exemplified by American Indians and natives of the Pacific islands recently "discovered" by the English explorer Captain Cook. The fact that these peoples lived in harmony with nature, unencumbered by the trappings of civilization, intrigued intellectuals. They viewed these "noble savages" as living in an ideal state. Clearly a trend away from the contrived and toward simplicity was in the air.

Brown obliged his clients by turning the grounds of their country estates into parks with large expanses of grass, tranquil ponds, and trees artfully placed either in clumps or singly. Some of Brown's contemporaries enhanced such landscapes with "ruins" seemingly left over from classical times but actually erected at the landscape designer's direction for the purpose of adding a picturesque note. To their owners these gardens represented nature in a gentle mood.

The influence of these English parks is seen in the design of Central Park in New York City and of municipal parks throughout the United States. Frederick Law Olmsted designed Central Park in 1858 in conjunction with Calvert Vaux. Olmsted also designed parks in this mode in many other American cities, as well as parkways, suburban communities, cemeteries, and campuses. He is credited with making landscape architecture a recognized profession in the United States.

Modern landscape design often shows influences from the Orient, particularly from China and Japan. The gardens and paintings of these cultures gave Westerners an increased appreciation of the aesthetic qualities of the structure and textures of plants and rocks. Muslim gardens, such as those of Persia and the Alhambra in Spain, reinforce our awareness of the delights of water.

## What Landscape Designers Do

The materials with which a landscape designer works are obvious: earth, plants, water, rocks, building and paving materials, and sometimes sculpture and even entire buildings. Today with many industrial sites being abandoned along waterfronts and inner cities, landscape designers are receiving commissions to convert these wastelands into viable open spaces for private and public use.

A landscape designer employs a bulldozer if a site needs extensive reshaping—perhaps to form a bank of earth to hide an unpleasant view or cut down noise from a road. When changing the contours of the earth, having the resulting forms blend with the surrounding landscape is an important consideration. If the plan requires more earth than the site provides, the landscape designer secures it from excavations elsewhere. Making a bank sounds like a big undertaking but proves cheaper than building a wall. A planting of shrubs and trees designed to serve as a screen takes perhaps ten years to reach maturity, while a bank planted with shrubs serves the purpose admirably from the day of installation.

A landscape designer chooses plants that thrive under the conditions presented by the site, keeping in mind which parts of the area will be sunny, which will have partial sun, and which will always be in shade, as these factors influence the choice of plants. In addition, when selecting plants, he or she chooses those whose sizes, colors, and textures are pleasing in combination. Increasingly, landscape designers choose plants native to the region where they are working, so their work will strengthen the local ecosystems.

Trees are usually an important part of the plan. Their height, silhouette, branching pattern, and the color and texture of their bark and leaves all contribute to the overall scheme. Moreover, trees cast welcome shade in the summertime. If the landscape designer chooses trees that are leafless in winter, he or she considers how those trees look at that time of year. A well-formed tree with bare branches seen against a wintry sky is just as beautiful, if not more so, than the same tree in summer with a full crop of leaves. Fortunately semimature trees transplant successfully, though transplanting them is expensive. On the other hand, young trees develop sooner than one might suppose.

Shrubs, flowers, and ground covers are other types of vegetation at a landscape designer's disposal. Shrubs provide intermediate heights between trees and ground covers and like trees offer interesting structure, color, and texture. Flowers serve as colorful accents. Grass as a ground cover provides an expanse of green that acts as an effective foil to other vegetation and, of course, gives a surface for walking or playing. Other ground covers also provide color as well as a variety of textures. Paving satisfactorily covers areas that receive considerable use.

Water—falling, flowing, leaping, or calm—increases the appeal of almost any site. In hot arid climates especially, the sight and sound of water conveys a sense of refreshing coolness. In temperate climates, landscape designers use water more lavishly, adding appeal to a tiny courtyard, a broad landscape, or anything in between. Plastic liners make possible pools and even lakes in places where these were not possible in times past.

Landscape designers sometimes place rocks of interesting shapes among vegetation or stand them apart like silent sentinels. Rocks can serve as a base for falling water, or, scattered in a channel of running water, they can cause the water to ripple and foam. Pebbles or larger stones sometimes act as ground cover. The solidness of rocks, their texture, and their usually subtle coloring contrast pleasingly with the relative airiness and mostly green coloring of plants and the limpid, elusive qualities of water.

In some cases a landscape designer provides a suitable setting for a structure or structures already in existence or beautifies a space between buildings. Sometimes a client wants a landscape designer to design structures such as pavilions, amphitheaters, playhouses, fountains, bridges, walls, fences, trellises, light fixtures, benches, or anything else desirable. Sometimes a site requires raised planting beds to protect plants or to provide sufficient soil depth for plants if the area covers a subterranean garage or something of the sort. Some clients agree to the purchase of a sculpture or sculptures, decorative urns, a sundial, birdbath, or well, thus adding focal points to beguile visitors. Planning for all such amenities comes within the province of the landscape designer.

In making a design for a particular site, a landscape designer keeps in mind the degree of maintenance that will be available for the completed project. Particularly helpful is developing a maintenance plan that relies on the local climate and seasonal cycles of nature. For instance, it is advisable to plant drought-resistant plants in the desert or salt-water tolerant vegetation in coastal wetland areas. He or she gives the client a management plan telling what to

do when, or installs an irrigation system and supplies site maintenance, so the site will remain attractive and in good repair.

Borders, hedgerows, and paths provide structure and can define
intimate spaces that seem like outdoor rooms. Benches and chairs
can provide places for reading, conversing, or meditating.

Following the example of the Japanese, some landscape designers provide special places for moon viewing. They also make certain that the completed landscape will present a pleasing prospect
from all viewpoints, including those from the windows of nearby
buildings. No detail capable of enhancing the pleasure of those who
will eventually use the area is too small for consideration.

Sometimes landscape designers make small-scale models to
demonstrate to their clients what they have in mind. These can be
made using the computer or actual physical materials.

A landscape designer can mold some substance such as putty to
indicate the contours of the site and then place within these contours miniature imitations of vegetation, which are available in specialty stores: small-scale trees of metal, hedges of plastic, and plastic
turf. Tiny twigs can be used to imitate leafless trees in winter, tiny
pebbles to indicate rocks, blue paper or plastic to imitate water. A
model makes it easier for a client to envision what the project will
look like when completed.

The concerns of landscape designers extend to our natural environment. They want the magnificence and beauty of the out-of-
doors preserved for the enjoyment of present and future generations.
To that end, they contract to make plans for the management of
forest and wilderness areas—plans that provide for the protection
of plants, wildlife, landforms, and other manifestations of nature.
They also suggest provisions for public use of such areas.

A landscape designer works alone, in association with other landscape designers, for a governmental agency, or in a multidisciplinary

design office involving architects and planning and engineering professionals as well as landscape designers. In any case, once a client and regulatory agencies approve a design, the landscape designer or others in the firm or agency see to it that the design materializes. To accomplish this, a landscape designer deals with many different individuals, including people from nurseries, workers to do the planting, perhaps earth movers, building contractors, masons, paving specialists, plumbers, electricians, sculptors, and others. The involvement of so many skills makes for a complicated process, but for the landscape designer the process is a truly creative one well worth the effort involved.

Lawrence Halprin, who is based in San Francisco, is considered the preeminent landscape designer in the United States. He was given the responsibility of designing the Franklin Delano Roosevelt Memorial in Washington, DC, which stands in a seven-and-a-half-acre triangle formed by the Jefferson, Lincoln, and Washington Memorials. Halprin planned this memorial as a series of four "rooms." Each room represents an epoch in FDR's administration, from the Great Depression to his funeral and the end of World War II. Incorporated into an environment of waterfalls, rough granite outcroppings, and reflecting pools are artworks by George Segal, Robert Graham, and Leonard Baskin.

## How to Get Started in Landscape Design

To qualify as a landscape architect, one must attend a college or university that offers a degree in this field. Required studies include art history, environmental and social sciences, language, mathematics, construction techniques, and studio work in landscape design and planning. Some states require that landscape architects secure a license.

Not all landscape designers study landscape design in a college or university before embarking on a career in this field. Deborah Nevins studied architectural history at Columbia University and taught landscape history at Barnard College. Her first assignment in landscape design resulted from a landscape design lecture she gave at Cooper Hewitt, the Smithsonian's museum of design in New York City. A couple in the audience was so intrigued with Nevins's ideas that they asked her to landscape the grounds of a house they owned in Connecticut. So Nevins undertook her first assignment as a landscape designer. (The grounds were a former golf course!) Her clients were pleased with the result, and several of their friends so admired Nevins's work that they asked her to undertake projects for them. Nevins's career as a landscape designer took off, and she now travels the United States and beyond overseeing landscaping projects both large and small. Nevins is based in New York City.

The median salary of landscape designers in 2002 was about $47,400. The middle 50 percent earned between $36,140 and $62,470. The lowest 10 percent earned less than $28,730 and the highest 10 percent earned more than $79,620.

Architectural, engineering, and related services employed more landscape designers than any other group of industries, and there the median annual earnings were $46,980 in 2002. Anyone who loves nature and has an artistic bent would surely get a great deal of satisfaction if he or she chose landscaping as a career.

# 12

# METALWORKING

Artists who work with metal use a variety of metals and methods. Metals they use include iron, copper, bronze, brass, steel, aluminum, lead, silver, gold, titanium, tin, and stainless steel. Their methods include forging, hammering, spinning, bending, casting, electroforming, and assembling.

Traditionally a blacksmith softened iron to a red-hot state in a furnace fueled with coal, laid the glowing metal on the anvil, and with mighty blows from a hammer shaped the metal. During the process, whenever the metal cooled, it was returned to the fire until it became red-hot again and thus once more malleable. The iron used was called *wrought iron*.

Today most metalsmiths have brick-lined furnaces heated with gas. In place of wrought iron, they usually use different kinds of steel—alloys of iron and varying amounts of carbon. They heat the metal to a glowing red and then chill it in water, oil, or air, depending upon the alloy they are using. The metal is then tempered to reduce its hardness and to acquire the degree of toughness necessary for the project at hand. Tempering means reheating the steel to a temperature below the glowing state. Some present-day metalworkers forge metal in the old way; others substitute the heat of a torch for the heat of a furnace. The temperature needed, again, depends upon the alloy being used. The lower the heat, the harder the steel.

## What Metalworkers Do

Artists who work in metal usually make drawings or models in clay beforehand to serve as guides. Sometimes, however, the best ideas come during the course of the work. For that reason an artist sometimes articulates only the basic forms on a preliminary drawing or model and depends upon further inspiration coming when the material is malleable, ready to take on whatever form the artist wishes. From metal an artist may forge door knockers and hinges, drawer pulls, andirons, fire screens and fireplace tools, lighting fixtures, candlesticks, bookends, gates, railings, grilles, weather vanes, garden lanterns, bowls, pitchers, teapots, goblets, tumblers, and more—even beds, tables, chairs, and benches.

Copper was the first metal used by man. Later cultures discovered that bronze, a combination of copper and tin, serves admirably as a material for tools, weapons, and art. Somewhere along the line, metalsmiths combined copper and zinc to produce brass. From copper, brass, silver, gold, and aluminum, artists shape bowls, trays, coffee and tea services, casseroles, jugs, candleholders, plaques, and jewelry by cold forging with hammers and stakes.

Except for aluminum, they heat these materials periodically during the work and then allow the metal to cool before resuming work. This process of heating and then cooling is called *annealing*. Annealing keeps the metal from becoming brittle.

To produce the various items they turn out, metalsmiths use so-called stakes. These stakes have the form their name suggests and heads of various shapes. Their diversity allows the artist to choose a stake whose head size and shape correspond to the curve or angle that the artist wishes to impart to the metal. The artist inserts a stake in a block of hardwood or clamps it in a vise to hold it steady. Ready-made stakes are of iron; for a particular task an artist may make one of wood.

Say the objective is a round shallow bowl. The artist first cuts a round piece of sheet metal. Then in the method of cold forging called *raising*, the artist holds an area of the outer edge of the round piece of metal against the round head of a stake. The artist hammers that particular area, then repeatedly shifts the sheet metal to hammer each area along the outer edge against the stake, giving each spot the same number of blows. Next the artist hammers a band just inside that previously worked, then does the same for succeeding bands until the whole piece has been hammered. The artist repeats this process over and over until achieving the shape wanted. Sometimes a metalsmith uses different size hammers and changes the stake a time or two during the process. In the last stage a planishing hammer (a hammer with a slightly convex face) wielded lightly evens the surface.

Artists also shape metal by a method called *sinking*. In this method, the metal is "sunk" into the shape desired rather than raised. The artist places a piece of sheet metal on a sandbag or on a piece of wood hollowed to the desired shape and directs the blows to what will be the inner side of the object rather than to the outer side, as is the case in raising.

To work on a large form, an artist suspends a metal sheet, either enclosed loosely in a frame or not, thus making it possible to direct blows to either side. The sheet is flipped over when the artist wants to direct blows to the other side. In another method of working on a large form, the artist lays the metal sheet horizontally between two supports and when wanting to work on the other side, flips the sheet over.

Seamless, hollow bowls made by raising or sinking range from shallow forms and hemispheres to nearly closed spheres. Artists also form cylindrical, conical, and oval shapes in this way.

Metalsmiths also can make rounded or oval vessels of copper, brass, German silver, or aluminum on a spinning lathe. In this process a round piece of wood called a *chuck* is mounted on the lathe and sheet metal of the proper size is clamped to the chuck. The metalsmith shapes the vessel as the lathe rotates by continually changing the shape of the chuck until the chuck eventually has the shape the completed piece will have, and by pressing the sheet against the chuck with rounded, polished steel tools. During the shaping the artist occasionally anneals the metal sheet (except for aluminum) to return it to a nonbrittle state. Forming a vessel on a spinning lathe is a creative act in that the metalsmith fashions the chuck and by applying pressure brings the metal sheet to the desired shape.

Artists can make angular shapes by bending rather than hammering. Sometimes, however, they hammer such objects as a finishing process to give the surfaces a hammered look. Angular shapes require seams; artists make these by soldering, riveting, or hemming. They also attach components such as handles, feet, and bases by soldering or riveting. These components either can reflect the object's outline or contrast with it.

The kind of soldering used in creative metalwork is called *hard soldering*. In this process, binding wire or clamps hold the edges to be joined in place. The solder, in the form of a rod, a thin strip, or snippets, is usually an alloy of the metal of the work and another metal. Obviously the solder must melt at a lower temperature than the metal being joined. The artist places solder along the edges of the pieces to be joined and then heats the work and the solder with a torch. The molten solder flows between the edges of the pieces to be joined. A substance called *flux*, usually borax, is used with the solder to prevent the formation of an oxide film on the metal during the heating. When the artist removes the heat, the solder hardens, bonding the edges.

Riveting is an acceptable way of joining copper, brass, aluminum, or iron. Metalsmiths may use rivets in decorative ways, forming simple patterns with them or combining them with other elements to form patterns. Small objects are cold riveted; larger ones require heat.

In the technique of joining metal edges called *hemming*, a metalsmith folds the edges and interlocks the folds either flat or rounded. The metalsmith either makes the tools for this process or buys them.

Another time-honored method of producing metal objects, particularly of bronze, is that of casting. To make a cast metal object, the artist first prepares a model, using any one of a variety of materials: plaster, wax, Styrofoam, clay, or wood. Or an artist uses as a model something formed by nature, for instance a feather or a dead animal.

Though some artists do their own casting, others delegate the casting to workers in a foundry. Either way, a mold is made from the model and molten metal poured into the mold. After the metal hardens, the object is released from the mold and finished by filing rough spots, if that seems desirable, and in the case of bronze, perhaps by applying acids to create an attractive patina.

More metalsmiths use their skills to create jewelry than anything else. Most often their material is either silver or gold. Usually they do their own casting. They form the shape in wax and then cast it in metal by the lost-wax method. Jewelers and other metalworkers also use the techniques of engraving, etching, and chasing to decorate metal objects. Engraving means cutting a design into metal with a sharp tool. In etching, acid eats a design into the metal. In chasing, punches and a mallet force the design into the metal.

Many contemporary metal sculptors work directly with metal rather than casting sculptures. Metal sheets, rods, pipes, and wires comprise their materials. They cut metal with tin cutters or a welding torch, bend metal over a piece of wood or other material to get the shape they want, or work without such aids. Sculptors assemble metal parts by slotting, riveting, screwing, gluing, soldering, or welding.

Welding means bonding two pieces of metal by hammering them together while the metal is white-hot. For bonding metals other than iron, sculptors use a welding torch to bring the metal to a white-hot state. For iron, only the old-time forging method of joining pieces by hammering them in white heat is considered satisfactory, as using a torch to melt iron creates shapeless bulges. White heat has a temperature higher than that of red heat.

Artists sometimes solder or weld wires or thin strips of sheet metal and shape them over a mold to form sculptures. In such sculptures, open space often alternates with the wire or metal strips to give an airy feeling.

Another way of shaping metal is by electroforming, a process in which metal is deposited into a mold by electrical means. When the metal has solidified, the piece is released from the mold. The use of a mold makes possible the making of exact duplicates. Wax or rubber molds can produce curvilinear shapes not possible when metal is shaped with a hammer.

Some sculptors use so-called found pieces of metal to make sculptures—that is, pieces of metal found in, say, a junkyard, a secondhand shop, or the artist's studio. A sculptor uses these in ways different from their original purposes. John Chamberlain hammered and compressed auto parts such as fenders and bumpers to create sculptures. On close examination, the face of a Picasso sculpture of a gorilla turns out to be a toy auto. In Picasso's sculpture titled *Bull's Head*, he used a bicycle seat to represent the head of a bull and a bicycle's handlebars for the horns.

A sculptor who works with metal probably conceives a plan before beginning but may digress from the plan as the work progresses, trying out different ideas and taking advantage of fortuitous accidents. This freedom is comparable to that enjoyed by an abstract expressionist painter.

Often a sculpture made with metal resembles nothing from reality, though it possibly suggests a recognizable creature or object, either vaguely or in a straightforward manner. Artists may incorporate movement into such sculptures with power supplied by a motor, a passing breeze, or the viewer. Often a spirit of humor is involved. The aim is to appeal to the imagination rather than to create beauty.

A sculptor who makes a metal sculpture for an outdoor setting must consider the effects of weathering. Stainless steel and aluminum are suitable for this purpose, as weather doesn't affect them adversely. Corten steel left outdoors develops one coating of rust, then no more. Because the rust gives color, some regard the rust as an asset. Other metals placed outdoors require protective coatings.

## Using Your Metalworking Skills

A market exists for artworks of metal not only for restorations of venerable buildings but also for new structures, as the severity of much twentieth-century architecture makes an excellent background for metal artworks. Consequently, metalsmiths often receive commissions to create suitable accoutrements for buildings of contemporary design, particularly churches. The bold quality of works of art in metal makes a strong statement in such surroundings.

Artists may combine different metals and also different ways of working with metal in the same piece. Albert Paley, whom most authorities consider to be our era's preeminent metalsmith, created twelve-hundred-pound gates of forged steel, brass, bronze, and copper for the Renwick Gallery in Washington, DC. New York State commissioned him to create a pair of gates for the Senate chamber in the statehouse in Albany as part of a program to restore the statehouse to its former splendor. Paley forged and fabricated mild steel, bronze, and brass into handsome gates that are without question works of art.

The metalwork of Robert Butler, whose studio is in the Hudson River Valley, has earned a place in the Boston Museum of Fine Arts. One of Butler's specialties is the production of silver-gilt wine coasters that have an intricate oak-leaf-and-acorn pattern produced in a mold he made. Once the coasters are formed, he continues to work the silver to create a high gloss. His coasters are sold in some of the finest jewelry stores.

The beguiling surfaces and graceful contours of handcrafted metal objects make them unforgettable. Like alchemists of old, metalsmiths can bring to pass seeming magic. Angelo Garro, one of a considerable number of metalsmiths in San Francisco who specialize in handcrafted metal objects, says "There will always be people who want to possess something individually crafted of metal. There is still a real appreciation for it. The actual work is easy for me and always very rewarding."

The making of large metalworks is not solely an undertaking for males. In Sonoma County, California, Jackie Kennedy is part of the renaissance in metalworking. She lives on a 150-acre ranch where she cultivates vintage English rose varieties, which are mostly climbing roses. She hated the kinds of trellises she found in stores except for very expensive ones in specialty shops, so she undertook to make her own. There was scrap metal lying around the ranch, and her husband had an arc welder. He showed her the basics of using the welder, and she found she liked working with metal. Now she has a fully equipped metal shop on the ranch and turns out trellises, gates, and fence panels that grace wine country estates, plant nurseries, and public housing projects.

Artists who work in metal can receive high prices for the works they produce. High prices are justified because producing them is labor intensive. They may sell them for up to $30,000 a piece. Metal objects that are comparatively small are sold through art galleries, shops that specialize in handcrafted items, and fairs. Large metal sculptures are usually commissioned.

# 13

---

# NEEDLEWORK

NEEDLE AND THREAD are among the most basic of civilization's tools. With them, items both functional and artistic have been created throughout the ages.

## History of Needlework

History doesn't record a time when needles didn't exist. Probably a thorn or splinter of wood, bone, or ivory with a hole pierced through it served as the first needle. Our Stone Age ancestors no doubt used such needles to lace together pelts with sinew or animal hair, thereby providing themselves protection from rain and cold. After a while they undoubtedly used needles and sinew or animal hair to ornament clothing as well as to hold it together.

Egyptian tomb paintings show decorations on tents, couch covers, clothing, and hangings that appear to have been made with needle and thread. Paintings on Greek vases show clothing apparently embellished with embroidery. The Romans so esteemed needlework they called it "painting with thread"—an apt description.

Through the centuries needlework enhanced the prestige of church and state. In the Middle Ages the clergy wore vestments completely covered with embroidery. Monks and nuns embroidered these vestments and also sumptuous church cloths. Members of the imperial households of China wore silk robes embroidered with silk thread in magnificent patterns. In eleventh-century France, needle-workers commemorated the defeat of Harold of England by William the Conqueror by embroidering a narrative scroll 231 feet long and 19½ inches wide. This remarkable work, still in good condition, is exhibited in Bayeaux, France. It is called the Bayeaux Tapestry, but it is actually embroidery.

In former times embroiderers organized into guilds. In sixteenth-century and seventeenth-century London, the Borders' Company enjoyed high esteem. In Greece in the eighteenth century, the gilt embroiderers held first place among the guilds, accumulated the most wealth, and attracted the most members.

In time homemakers began to embroider. In Russia and Central Europe the style of elaborately embroidered clothing often indicated the region from which the wearer came. In addition to clothing, homemakers embroidered towels, window curtains, coverings for upholstered furniture, bed valances, bed curtains, bedspreads, and other items.

In colonial America most girls and some boys learned to embroider. The usual first effort, a sampler, exhibited different kinds of stitches tracing the forms of numerals, alphabets in different styles, and the name and birth date of the maker. Sometimes a sampler included an embroidered picture of the family home, flowers, trees, birds, and animals. Oftentimes a pious verse or sentiment supposedly revealed the maker's thoughts. Some of these samplers have come down to us as charming reminders of the importance of needlework in bygone times.

## What Needlework Artists Do

Today anyone who aspires to become an artist whose specialty is needlework will probably first practice stitches, just as the creators of samplers were doing when they devised their creations. Knowing just a few simple stitches enables one to make handsome embroideries, though many different stitches are possible. Some of the better-known stitches bear names like running stitch, stem stitch, back stitch, cross-stitch, long and short stitch, Romanian stitch, Cretan stitch, and feather stitch.

Crewel embroidery is embroidery done with wool on any fabric. Crewelwork goes fairly quickly as the thickness of wool yarn negates the possibility of dainty stitches. Also the design of crewel embroidery, usually large and flowing, leaves considerable open space. Anyone doing crewel embroidery usually employs a frame to hold the cloth taut. Traditionally crewel-embroidered cloth has served as bed curtains, bedspreads, hangings, and coverings for chair seats and backs, footstools, and loose cushions.

Needlepoint, usually done with wool thread, covers a square-meshed canvas. The canvas for needlepoint comes in different size meshes. The type of needlepoint called *petit point* employs the smallest mesh, regular needlepoint uses a slightly larger mesh, *gros point* a still larger mesh, and *large gros* point the largest mesh. A person making a needlepoint piece completely covers the canvas with threads so that they become as one with the backing rather than being a surface decoration.

The basic needlepoint stitches are the continental, flame, half-cross, and basket weave, though one can make an attractive pattern with only two or three stitches. A finished needlepoint piece requires blocking. Blocking means straightening the piece and perhaps stretching it to align it properly. Shops that sell needlepoint supplies do professional blocking, as well as usually conducting classes in needlepoint.

Items made with needlepoint last almost indefinitely. Martha Washington stitched twelve needlepoint seat cushions in a shell design for Mount Vernon. Some of the cushions survive in their original setting. For anyone who wishes to make, or have made, something to pass down as an heirloom, an item made of needlepoint is a good choice. One woman needlepointed a stairway runner that gives a brief, pictorial account of colonial American history, a treasure worthy of being handed down through generations.

Needlepoint can be used to make chair and ottoman covers, pillow covers, rugs, wall hangings, picture frames, drapery valances, handbags, eyeglass containers, yokes for denim jackets, handbags, belts, even slippers.

Needlepoint shops carry a huge array of needlepoint patterns printed or hand-painted on needlepoint mesh in color. Subjects include floral designs, Turkish and Oriental rug patterns, abstract designs, copies of masterpiece paintings, dog portraits, and most anything one can think of. Many shops will create or can commission custom-ordered canvases—perhaps a client's favorite painting, photo, or a fabric or wallpaper pattern. Or you can paint a design of your own devising on needlepoint mesh. People so inclined can even devise needlepoint patterns on their computers.

Other embroidery techniques bear names like drawn-thread work, hardanger, smocking, and fagoting. In drawn-thread work, one pulls bands of threads from cloth and then draws threads running in the opposite direction together into groups to form patterns. The result can look like a piece of exquisite lace. In the hardanger technique, embroidery thread is satin-stitched in blocks that often outline cutout squares. Smocking, which is embroidery on top of gathers, works best on fabrics with a regular pattern. Fagoting uses embroidery stitches to join two edges of cloth in an open lacy pattern.

Appliqué is a method of decoration that involves sewing fabric shapes onto a larger fabric. The French artist Henri Matisse designed vestments and altar cloths for a chapel in Vence, France, that feature appliquéd designs in violets, greens, lemon yellows, poppy reds, and blacks. Appliqué also provides a way of enhancing the beauty of quilts, wall hangings, banners, and clothing. In the traditional way of appliquéing, one tucks under the edges of a fabric shape and then blind-stitches it to a background. Makers of present-day hangings sometimes expose the edges of appliquéd pieces, however, and possibly ravel the edges for textural interest.

Beadwork is also done with needle and waxed thread. Sometimes beadwork entirely covers an object. In this case, meshed canvas serves as the base. Sometimes beadwork decorates garments. Often beadworkers work their designs in cross-stitch. The beautiful beadwork done by North American Indians and exhibited in museums gives inspiration to anyone wishing to follow their example, as do the beaded purses ladies in the early part of the twentieth century carried when they went out in the evening to, say, the opera or an elegant restaurant. Some cities have shops devoted solely to selling beads. Craft and needlework shops often sell beads and magazines suggesting how one can use beads to create beautiful things.

Knitting needles differ from embroidery needles in that they lack an eye and are considerably longer and stouter than embroidery needles. A knitter places loops of yarn on one knitting needle and then draws additional loops through them with the aid of another knitting needle, thereby constructing a fabric that can be open and lace-like, dense enough for a rug, or anything in between.

Knitters primarily fashion garments, particularly sweaters, but they also make afghans and even sculptures. Yarn shops sell beautiful yarns in every imaginable luscious hue, an array dazzling enough to coax almost anyone to take up knitting. Magazines devoted to the art of knitting print patterns for items to be knit. One of the advantages of knitting is that a work in the making is portable; you can take your knitting with you almost anywhere you need to go.

One crochets with thread and a hook. In some cultures, indigenous people know how to make a chain by interlocking loops of string with their fingers. This practice probably led to crocheting. Someone introduced the use of a hook as a refinement. Probably wood or bone provided the material for the first crochet hooks; today they are made of steel or wood. To most people the word *crochet* brings to mind doilies, bedspreads, and tablecloths our great-grandmothers crocheted of cotton thread.

Crocheters today turn out creations the like of which our great-grandmothers and those who went before them probably never dreamed of: abstract hangings, necklaces, intricately patterned coats, capes, jackets, vests, skirts, dresses, and sculpture. Classes in crocheting are held in some needlework shops. Magazines and books available in such shops are another means of learning how to crochet and are also a source of patterns.

Many people believe that knitting and crocheting, both of which use only one continuous thread, were invented by Arabs, as the oldest extant specimens were found in Egyptian tombs of the Arab period. These specimens are not earlier than the seventh or eighth century A.D.

Related to crocheting is tatting, a way of making handmade lace formed usually by looping and knotting with a single cotton thread and a small shuttle.

Some people employ needlework techniques to make handsome rugs. Knitted and crocheted rugs impart a country look to a room, while rugs made with embroidery stitches, using heavy wools on a burlap base, present a more refined appearance. Many people prize needlepoint rugs above all others. Rya rugs evolved from Scandinavian bed coverings that were used with the pile side down. When woven blankets became available, Scandinavians flipped over their ryas and used them as floor coverings. Originally Scandinavians wove ryas; now makers of rya rugs sew them, using sturdy linen or rug burlap as the base. They usually select wool yarn for the pile, though strips of cloth sometimes substitute. The only tool needed is a rug needle with a large eye. One works rows of knots, leaving loops of the desired length on the right side, and then cuts the loops to form a deep pile.

Hangings made with stitchery techniques run the gamut from whimsical to handsome. In making a hanging, an artist creates a kind of picture, either representational or abstract. Sometimes the artist leaves the fabric background as it is, other times paints it, silk-screens a pattern on it, batiks it, tie-dyes it, enhances it with a photographic image, or treats it in any way desired, then embellishes the hanging with embroidery, needlepoint, or just plain everyday running stitches made by hand or machine.

Sometimes makers of hangings incorporate appliqué into their work, possibly padding the appliqué. Sometimes they quilt the whole hanging or parts of it for a three-dimensional effect. Sometimes an artist attaches objects to a hanging: beads, buttons, feathers, shells, pods, pieces of leather or wood, ceramics, pasta, and so forth. The results often prove stunning.

Other needlework artists create soft sculptures of fabric or other supple material such as vinyl. Valerie Snyder of California made fabric animal puppets for her elementary class; then by adding zippers, she converted her creations into purses and travel bags. She and her sister, Priscella Snyder of New York, developed a thriving business producing and selling sculptural bags of all sizes in the forms of dogs, cats, dragons, cranes, grasshoppers, cows, elephants, mice, harlequins, geishas, ballerinas, and most anything else.

Other needlework artists make soft sculptures with an inner support system of chicken wire. This support makes possible soft sculptures of considerable size.

Needlework artists find inspiration for designs almost everywhere in nature, books and magazines, architectural details, memories, the sights that greet one at every turn. They use inspiration as a starting point; then they let their imaginations take over.

To make a guide for stitchery, one can draw or paint a design freehand on fabric; use ruler, compass, and cutout shapes; or plot the design on plain or graph paper and transfer it to fabric with nonsmear carbon paper or a pantograph. A pantograph is a device used to make an enlargement or reduction of a design, or copy it in the same size. Pantographs are available at art supply stores.

Some needlework artists transfer a design by pricking holes along the lines of the original, either with an unthreaded sewing machine or the lower half of a needle set into the eraser of a pencil. They rub powdered charcoal or powdered chalk through the pricked holes and then paint the lines suggested by the powder with watercolor to serve as guides.

Many other methods are available to needlework artists for transferring a design. Some artists fold paper into fourths or eights, make cutouts, unfold the paper, and transfer the resulting design to fabric. Sometimes artists draw or paint only the basic lines of a design on fabric as a guide for stitching, then fill in the rest with freehand stitching. Some artists just begin and go on from there; they find a spirit of freedom and willingness to experiment to be assets.

One young woman, Mary Hall, made colorful banners to hang outside her home—one for each month of the year, each with a motif appropriate to the month in which it was to be hung. Friends asked her to make banners to hang outside their homes with motifs that referred to their names, holidays, or special interests. Soon she had a business going. Such banners are also used to hang outside shops as a means of announcing the kind of shop that lies within. Banners are also hung from lampposts to announce the confines of a street fair or to proclaim the eminent arrival of a festival of some sort. Churches and other organizations sometimes commission banners to hang over or near their entrances.

Mary Hall also made herself a tote bag that was admired by sunbathers on a Florida beach. Some of them asked her to make unusual bags for them, evidence that needlework artists can find their art not only an absorbing pursuit but also a financially rewarding one.

## How to Get Started in Needlework

Many craft shops offer classes in various types of needlework, or you could teach yourself with the aid of books. If you can't find publications with instructions for the kind of needlework that is of interest to you, try the shop called Hard-to-Find Needlework Books; its website is http://www.needleworkbooks.com, and it lists more than a hundred titles.

People the world over appreciate needlework that beautifies homes, glorifies places of worship, and creates distinctive clothing and items that make handsome gifts. Some needleworkers sell their creations through gift shops that are cooperative ventures organized by artists as a place to sell their wares. Needleworkers also sell the items they make at fairs or advertise them in publications. If their needlework skills are known, they may be commissioned to produce needlework for special purposes.

# 14

# PAINTING

PAINTING IS ONE of the oldest and most expressive of the arts. Most people enjoy looking at and even owning paintings. They get much pleasure from the beauty and emotions that paintings elicit. Painters, too, experience much satisfaction and pleasure in creating their works of art.

## History of Painting

People have painted images on many different kinds of surfaces using a variety of mediums for at least thirty-seven thousand years. Paintings that old still adorn the walls and ceilings of caves in Spain and southern France. Through the thousands of years that our predecessors roamed the earth in search of food, they also left behind paintings on numerous rock surfaces. Many of these survive. These paintings reveal information about the people of bygone days, the objects they used, and their customs.

Our prehistoric ancestors ground minerals to get colors. They combined the ground minerals with fat or other substances to make paint. Probably they applied their paint with fingers, feathers, frayed twigs, fur pads, and brushes made of fiber or hair. They also blew paint onto surfaces through hollow bird bones. Their representations of animals, plants, and humans show surprising skill.

For the most part, ancient artists gave up rock art after settling in villages, though the present-day graffiti one sees on exterior walls counts as a descendant of early rock art. Once people settled in villages and cities, they began to paint on the ceilings and interior and exterior walls of their dwellings. They also decorated their pottery, clothing, furniture, and other possessions with painted scenes and designs. We continue to do this today.

## What Painters Do

Artists today still use paints whose pigments come from minerals; they also use paints chemically formulated in factories. Some methods of applying paint remain much the same as those used long ago. Today, however, artists buy their brushes or other means of applying paint in stores, rather than devising them themselves.

Parents and teachers often give children watercolors for their first painting experience. Painting with watercolors seems appropriate for children because watercolors are easy to use and to clean up. Actually watercolor is a difficult medium, for once a brush carrying watercolor touches paper, the paint clings, refusing to depart should the painter wish to make a change. Painting with watercolors requires forethought, care, and patience.

The choice of paper is important when painting with watercolors. Professional watercolorists usually choose thick, grained paper handmade from rags. The texture of such paper adds to the attractiveness of the finished work. The artist dampens the paper before starting to paint, perhaps putting it in a frame or taping it to a firm surface to keep the paper from wrinkling as it dries. To build up the picture, the artist applies successive color washes to the dampened paper. Unpainted patches of the paper represent light areas. After the paper dries, the artist adds accents and, if desired, lines. Watercolor paintings usually appear airy and delicate due to any unpainted areas and the transparency of watercolor. Watercolor also is used to tint drawings.

Gouache, also called poster paint, is an opaque watercolor paint. It dries almost immediately and gives a dull finish without any brush strokes in evidence. Gouache comes in a thick state, but if diluted, makes a wash. Gouache makes possible crisp lines and a suedelike finish. The artists who painted delicate Islamic and East Indian miniatures used gouache.

Renaissance painters invented oil paint, a favorite medium of painters ever since. Oil paint is made by mixing pigment with oil, usually linseed oil. It is not transparent unless greatly thinned. Its usual thickness makes it possible to build up the paint on the painting surface for an interesting texture. Oil paint dries slowly, so if an artist wishes to make a change before the paint has dried, the paint can be scraped off and the area repainted.

Most painters who use oil paint apply it to canvas stretched over a frame, but some artists use other fabrics, processed boards, wooden planks, bark, glass, or almost anything suitable as a ground for their paint. Artists usually give canvas a coat of sizing, a preparation usually made of glue, flour, varnish, or resins that fills the pores of the canvas. Sizing keeps the paint from sinking in and the edges of colored areas from blurring. Some artists like the look they get with unsized canvas, as color applied to unsized canvas sinks into the canvas and appears to be part of the canvas rather than lying on the surface. When an artist uses unsized canvas, the process is called *staining* rather than painting.

Acrylic paint is a combination of pigment and acrylic resin, a synthetic substance. Artists find working with acrylic paint much like working with oil paint and apply it to the same surfaces as are used for oil paint. Artists thin acrylic paint to make it transparent or use it as it comes from the tube. It differs from oil paint in that it dries quickly. Some artists prefer acrylic paint to oil paint because you don't need to use turpentine to clean up. Acrylic paint cleans up with water.

Casein paint, much used in ancient Rome and which is recently in favor with some modern artists, is a combination of pigment, lime, water, and the curd of cheese or milk. It comes in a liquid state, so it is sold in jars. It serves for making thin washes on cardboard, wood, and plaster walls or for a thick texture. Casein paint dries quickly.

Tempera reigned as the most favored medium of painters until the introduction of oil paint. True tempera combines pigment, water, and the yolks of fresh eggs, or sometimes instead of yolks, egg whites or the whole egg. Substances similar to egg sometimes substitute for it, but egg tempera is the most durable. Tempera comes in a liquid state, so it is sold in jars. Tempera gives a tough smooth surface with a satin sheen. Ancient Egyptians used tempera for painting mummy cases, papyrus rolls, and murals. Early Christians used it to decorate their catacombs and later Christians to ornament manuscripts, altarpieces, and icons. Some present-day artists paint with tempera.

When an artist is using oil or acrylic paint, he or she prepares for painting by squeezing dabs of color from tubes onto a palette. A traditional palette is a thin piece of wood with rounded corners and a thumbhole, but any shape will do. Today palettes are made of glass, metal, and plastic as well as wood.

An artist usually owns several brushes to avoid the necessity of cleaning a brush every time he or she wants to use a different color. Brushes come in different sizes adaptable to different uses. A painter keeps a container of turpentine and one of linseed oil nearby to use for thinning the paint. Or, an artist can use a palette knife to apply paint. A palette knife has a wooden handle and a flexible metal blade. A palette knife makes it possible to easily apply paint thickly.

Artists devise ways of applying paint other than with a brush or palette knife. Jackson Pollock placed his canvases on the floor and dripped, poured, or slung paint on them. The latter action created swirls of color. Or he splattered paint from a brush. He sometimes used a trowel or stick to maneuver the paint once it was on the canvas. Jules Olitski sprayed paint onto his canvases. Morris Louis poured paint onto unsized canvases. It appears that perhaps he pleated or folded some canvases before applying paint and used a stick to guide the paint. During one phase of Niki de Saint Phalle's career, she would arrange cans of spray paint in front of a canvas and shoot at the spray cans with a rifle so that paint bled onto the canvas!

Experimentation continues unabated. Some artists wish to attach objects to their painting surfaces. Julian Schnabel dotted his heavily painted canvases with shards of crockery. Distinctions between painting and sculpture sometimes become blurred, as when underpinnings project parts of a canvas into space, making a work three-dimensional.

Painting pictures to be hung on walls does not require a large investment in equipment nor a great deal of space for their execution. For many it proves an absorbing escape from the real world and a source of immeasurable pleasure as well as a means of income.

Interest in the ancient art of mural painting—painting on walls—was renewed in this country as a result of handsome murals created by the Mexican artists Diego Rivera, José Clemente Orozco, and David Alfaro Sigueiros. These artists worked in both Mexico and the United States in the early part of the twentieth century.

An artist plans a mural on a scale compatible with the building it will embellish. A mural on an exterior wall may be made by applying the paint to a dry surface or by using the fresco method.

When the paint is to be applied to a wall, the surface of the wall must first be cleaned, sealed, and primed. The design may then be transferred to the wall in one of three ways: It may simply be drawn on the wall freehand. Usually, however, the design is first drawn on paper, to a scale of perhaps one inch to one foot, and then one-foot squares are drawn onto the wall so that each square foot corresponds to a square inch of the sketch. The contents of each square inch of the sketch are then transferred to the corresponding square foot of wall in the appropriate dimensions. In this method several people can paint on the wall at the same time. If desired, any necessary changes or additions can be made later.

Usually acrylic paint is preferred for exterior murals. After the painting is finished, a coat of clear sealer is applied as protection against the elements and graffiti. If the surface is later defaced with graffiti, the graffiti can be removed with a solvent without removing the paint.

Another method of transferring a design for a mural to a wall is to project the sketch onto the wall and then trace the projected lines that make up the design onto the wall.

The fresco method of painting a mural was the method used by Michelangelo when he painted his now famous murals in the Sistine Chapel of the Vatican in Rome. Fresco is painting done on a freshly spread, moist, lime-plaster wall. In preparation, the artist begins with a full-scale drawing called a *cartoon*. The artist fastens the cartoon to the wall and presses the outlines of the cartoon into the damp plaster with a bone or metal stylus. Using the outlines in the plaster as a guide, the artist applies paint made from powdered pigments mixed with water. The lime in the plaster combines with the paint, so that when the plaster dries, the paint is an integral part of the wall surface.

If the wall for which a mural is planned is an interior wall, the paint may be applied to the dry surface of the wall, the fresco method of making a mural may be used, or the artist may paint the mural on canvas. In the latter case, after the paint on the canvas has dried, the artist takes the canvas off its frame, rolls it up, takes it to the site, restretches it on a frame, and fastens the frame to the wall or attaches the canvas to the wall with an adhesive.

A portable mural can be made using Masonite or marine ply-wood panels. Four-foot-by-eight-foot panels typically are used and are commonly grouped so as to form an eight-foot-by-sixteen or twenty-foot rectangle. They can be painted in a studio and then moved to wherever they are to be displayed. They are usually framed in the back and then can be bolted to a wall or hinged and given supports to hold them upright. Portable murals can be used as backdrops for rallies and speeches or stage productions.

In recent decades colorful murals appearing on a variety of structures have enlivened many cities and towns. In San Francisco a group called the Precita Eyes Muralists is responsible for scores of murals on both exterior and interior walls of public and commercial buildings, community centers, schools, recreation centers, and elsewhere. Its members sometimes even add interest to fences, including those surrounding construction sites. Murals painted by the Precita Eyes Muralists on or in public buildings are usually paid for by grants, while the owners of private property pay for murals painted on their property. The organization has two hundred members. At least eighty of these individuals are active muralists; the others give moral and financial support. The group also conducts workshops concerned with mural painting. Some of these workshops are for children and youth. Young people who attend these workshops participate on some projects.

Precita Eyes is a nonprofit organization, but the muralists get paid for their work. Perhaps such an organization exists in your community where you could learn mural painting skills that could lead to a means of livelihood.

The invention of the camera greatly influenced the course of painting. Mythological and historical subjects, portraits, still-life compositions, landscapes, and genre scenes traditionally comprised a painter's possible subjects. The camera excelled in portraying these subjects, except for mythological and historical subjects, so some artists began to produce other kinds of paintings. Rather than portraying reality, some artists create abstract art.

Abstract art may have barely recognizable elements of the real world but depends on the assumption that specifically aesthetic values reside in forms and colors. The paintings of other artists give no hint of reality. Sometimes such nonobjective paintings convey moods such as joy, sadness, calm, or foreboding. Others create physical sensations in the viewer by the juxtaposition of colors and shapes that seem to pull in opposite directions. The paintings of still others are simply design unencumbered by subject matter.

Shape, line, color, balance, and texture are a painter's primary concerns. Diagonal lines or repetition of form or color gives a sense of movement, while vertical and horizontal lines give a sense of calm and stability. Emphasis and unity also should be given consideration. When all these factors combine to form a pleasing composition, the result is art.

## Using Your Painting Skills

Anyone with painting skills can also utilize them in ways other than painting pictures to be hung on walls or creating murals.

Painting with stencils has recently become newly popular. Stencils allow one to decorate boxes, furniture, plaster walls, wood, glass, paper, floors, floor cloths, curtains, and other fabrics in much less time than it would take to do the project freehand.

Stenciling consists of applying paint with a stencil brush, sponge, or roller to the open spaces of a stencil. Stencils are made of Mylar, metal, or stiff paper. You can make your own stencils using freezer paper. Stencils made of freezer paper don't hold up as long as those made of sturdier materials, but they are satisfactory for small jobs.

A beginning stenciler may start by decorating a small box or picture frame or stenciling borders around a ceiling or doorway and then move on to more adventurous projects. Penny Burns of Glen Ellen, California, stenciled a lemon tree and a cat on a café wall for a client. Tanya Broussand of Pleasanton, California, enlivened her bedroom wall with a garden scene framed by trellises and ivy. The scene included a wrought-iron fence, a birdhouse, birds, and terracotta pots filled with plants. Pam Franklin used stencils to paint clouds and stars on the walls and ceiling of her baby's nursery.

When painting with a stencil, it is best to paint lightly so that the paint doesn't drip. Also the result is then more subtle and shaded. Freehand additions can be made to a design made with a stencil; the design then doesn't appear as rigid as it might otherwise.

In the past a stencil for every color used was needed, but today's fast-drying acrylic paints and removable painter's tape allow the work to proceed quickly and easily. Oil paints also can be used.

Perhaps you could establish a business giving new, unfinished furniture or furniture you purchased at secondhand stores a coat of paint, then decorating them with either stenciled or freehand designs and offering them for sale through a gift shop. The shop where your wares are offered for sale undoubtedly would want to be paid a commission for any sales.

Some shops that sell stencils give classes not only in stenciling but also on how to achieve decorative paint finishes, such as glazing, stippling, sponging, and wood graining. One could specialize in giving furniture such finishes or use these finishes as the background for stenciled or hand-painted designs. Such newly decorated items could be sold directly to the public or on commission through specialty shops.

Painting on glass is another way of using one's painting skills. You could purchase unadorned glass objects—glasses, goblets, plates, pitchers, vases, or anything else made of glass—and create designs on them with acrylic enamel paint. Once you have done this, baking them in a 325- to 350-degree household gas oven for half an hour makes the designs permanent so that they will withstand being washed in a dishwasher. Designs can be floral, geometric, plaid, checkerboard, polka dots, dashes, squiggles, stripes, anything you want. You could even apply gold leafing around the rims.

Look in the Yellow Pages of your telephone directory for firms that sell glassware wholesale that is suitable for painting. If such a firm doesn't exist in your area, you could order glassware from Mid-Atlantic of West Virginia, Inc., Old Route U.S. 50, Ellensboro, West Virginia 26346, telephone (304) 869-3351. If you request it, they will send you a catalog.

Another way to utilize painting skills is to produce painted floor cloths. Canvas floor cloths were used in colonial times by families who couldn't afford rugs. Sailors' wives made floor coverings from discarded sails. Today brightly colored floor cloths contribute to a casual, lived-in feeling. They don't absorb dust and can be easily sponged off, so they are ideal for allergy sufferers.

A floor cloth's design can imitate a marble or mosaic floor, reflect the design of a room's wallpaper, be a geometric or plaid design, anything a client wishes. A stencil of Mylar can serve as a means of applying the design to the canvas and freehand details can be added if wished.

Another area where painters use their skills is working as restorers of damaged and/or faded paintings. They use solvents to clean the surface, reconstruct or retouch damaged areas, and apply preservatives to protect the paintings. Training for this vocation is offered at some colleges and universities. The American Institute for Conservation of Historic and Artistic Works, 1717 K Street NW, Suite 301, Washington, DC, 20006, http://aic.stanford.edu, will send a list of such schools on receipt of a request. Art museums employ restorers, or one could work independently, getting clients by advertising in the Yellow Pages of telephone directories and getting referrals from art galleries that sell paintings, as people sometimes contact art galleries to learn where they can have paintings restored.

Training as a painter also can qualify one to be a consultant to a corporation or individual collecting art. Quite a few corporations have extensive art collections in their headquarters that they have acquired relying on the expertise of a knowledgeable artist when making purchases. The usual commission for such services is 10 percent of the cost of such purchases.

Some artists work in art administration in city, state, and federal arts programs. Others work as art critics, in art galleries, or are in charge of setting up art exhibits in museums.

Artists desiring to make their living from painting might have to supplement their income by teaching painting until such time as they have established a favorable reputation as an artist. Those with teaching certificates are eligible to teach in elementary or secondary schools; those with master's or doctoral degrees are qualified to teach in colleges or universities. Or you might give private lessons to individuals or groups.

Painting has long been considered one of the great arts. When most people hear the word *art*, paintings first come to mind. If you decide to become a painter, you will be joining the ranks of an esteemed profession.

# 15

# PERFORMANCE ART

PERFORMANCE ART IS a term used to describe performances put on by artists rather than actors. It can involve the audience, which is generally small, can occur in a variety of settings, and makes use of the immediate environment.

## History of Performance Art

The involvement of artists in performance goes back many centuries. In Renaissance times Leonardo da Vinci and other artists designed what they called *triumphs*, extravaganzas that took place in the streets and combined music, verse, costumes, and floats. Also during the Renaissance the great English architect Inigo Jones planned lavish entertainments that made use of a variety of arts for the enjoyment of the royal court.

During the first World War, Hugo Ball and Emmy Hennings, expatriate Germans, opened Cabaret Voltaire in Zurich as a place where they and their artist friends used their artistic skills to put on performances for their mutual pleasure. Posters and paintings hung on the walls. Artist Marcel Janco devised masks for the group. The masks called for costumes, so costumes were made. These programs included poetry reading, music, and dancing, often presented in ludicrous fashion. Ball, for instance, recited "sound poems"— verses without words—as though chanting a mass. Ball and his friend Richard Heulsenbeck chose the name Dada to describe the goings-on. "For Germans," Ball explained, "it [Dada] is a sign of foolish naïveté."

In Paris the surrealist movement superseded Dada. Surrealist artists staged performances that mixed their fascination with dreams and fantasy with the principles of simultaneity and chance espoused by the Dadaists. Ballet, music hall antics, film, and extraordinary costumes and decor were all parts of their productions. In a performance *Le jet de sang* (*The Jet of Blood*), presented by Antonin Artaud in 1927, a character called the "Whore" bit "God's hand" and an immense jet of "blood" shot across the stage. In the same year Artaud presented Roger Vitrac's *Les mystéres de l'amour* (*The Mysteries of Love*) in which the heroine shot a bullet into the audience, pretending to kill a spectator.

The Bauhaus, the German art school that operated in the twenties and early thirties, offered the first art school course in performance. Oskar Schlemmer, the director of performance activities, theorized that just as a two-dimensional painting might be transposed into a three-dimensional sculpture, performance could carry the process further by adding motion and sound to animate or inanimate "sculpture." In his *Figural Cabinet II*, metallic figures on wires dashed from background to foreground and back again. In another Bauhaus production a painting, *Tischegesellschaft*, came to life. For another performance Wassily Kandinsky illustrated Modest Mussorgsky's musical composition *Pictures at an Exhibition* with moveable colored forms and light projections. Pantomime, jazz bands, amazing costumes, satire, parody, the absurd, the grotesque, and pure pleasure were all parts of the proceedings. The so-called Bauhaus Festivities became famous and drew audiences from surrounding towns. Bauhaus performers even toured European cities.

One Bauhaus artist-teacher, Josef Albers, came to Black Mountain College in North Carolina. Albers told his students, "Art is concerned with the *how* and not the *what*. The performance—how it is done—that is the content of art." In 1936 he encouraged a former Bauhaus colleague, Zanti Schawinsky, to join the Black Mountain faculty. Schawinsky devised a stage studies program concerned with space, form, light, sound, movement, music, and time. His production *Spectrodrama* featured an interplay of light and geometric forms. His *Danse macabre*, a performance in the round in 1938, required the audience to wear masks and cloaks.

In the fall of 1959 Allan Kaprow, a student at the New School in New York City, sent out invitations for an event he called 18 Happenings in Six Parts. Arriving guests found a second-floor loft divided into three rooms by plastic walls covered with words, paint, collage, and rows of plastic fruit. Chairs for guests were arranged in circles and rectangles. Guests received cards explaining moves to make from room to room whenever a bell sounded. Ninety minutes of simultaneous happenings then ensued. Painters painted on canvases applied to the walls. Readers read from placards with mock solemnity. Other performers recited long series of monosyllabic words. Still others moved through physical sequences that were partly calisthenics and partly imitations of everyday activities. Music and other sounds reverberated through the rooms, and slides and films were projected onto walls—all in all, a bewildering array of activity.

The term *happening*, which Kaprow used to describe his event, henceforth described any multimedia event that supposedly just happened. Actually Kaprow carefully planned his happenings. Subsequent sponsors of happenings sometimes made detailed plans and sometimes did not. Often they left a great deal to chance and spontaneity. The intent of happenings ranged from amusement, nonsense, and mystification to political and social propagandizing.

## What Performance Artists Do

Performance art is the direct descendant of such happenings. Some describe performance art as events staged by artists. Some describe it as "live art"—that is, visual art plus sound and motion. Performance art, though closely related to theater, differs from theater in that it features artists presenting innovative spectacles, intriguing incidents, or anything else that occurs to them, while traditional theater features actors involved in character development and the acting out of a plot.

In 1992 at the groundbreaking ceremonies for the San Francisco Museum of Modern Art's new building, the Survival Research Laboratories, headed by Mark Pauline, staged a performance that involved a fiery spectacle and nerve-shattering noise. A flame-throwing cannon careened around the lot, and a sort of mortar spit out molten metal. These two contraptions together with a pair of giant pincers on wheels and an assemblage of many legs and a long metal arm attacked structures of cardboard and sheet metal. The event ended with an out-of-control fire, which the San Francisco Fire Department was called upon to quell. Pauline's purpose was to call attention to the violence in our high-tech world and our attraction to it.

One summer evening in 1995 about seven hundred people stood immobile on the grounds of Lincoln Center in New York City, peering through binoculars at scenes played out behind the forty windows of the nearby Radisson Empire Hotel that were visible from that vantage point. Headsets allowed those in the group to listen via radio to dialogues taking place within the rooms. What was seemingly a case of mass voyeurism was actually an audience viewing a piece of performance art called *C'est la vie*, which had been arranged by Véronique Guillard. Through one window they watched a seemingly steamy scene provided by a couple dressed in flesh-colored body stockings. Other actors played members of a Jewish family, a sleazy disc jockey, a dying invalid, and so on, providing the kinds of little dramas that might unfold in any New York City building. The performance was part of Lincoln Center's Summer Out of Doors festival.

Laurie Anderson and Meredith Monk win critical acclaim for their highly successful performance art. Each goes her own way, but together they have escalated performance art from an experimental activity restricted mostly to artists and their friends into a popular entertainment medium. In its beginnings performance art most often was a one-time event. These two, however, tour to major cities presenting their works to sizable audiences.

Laurie Anderson is an accomplished sculptor, photographer, and musician as well as a performance artist. Her first undertaking as a performance artist took place in Vermont, where she arranged for an "orchestra" of car horns to play a "symphony" of her devising in a drive-in band shell. In another early performance, she wore skates imbedded in ice and simultaneously played her violin and talked about the similarities between violin playing and skating, until the ice melted. Often her performances include songs of her own composition. Their words evoke images both amusing and disturbing. As she sing-speaks these songs, electronic filters distort her voice in strange ways or make it sound like the voice of a robot or vocoder.

Frequently films or slides made by Anderson serve as backdrops for her performances. In one episode of her performance *United States*, a double exposure of a photonegative likeness of the Statue of Liberty and an American flag spinning in a clothes dryer make it appear that flames engulf the hem of the statue's gown. Before this backdrop, Anderson tells of farmers whose silos store nuclear missile heads. From her electric violin she then elicits sounds like the wailing of sirens and the sobbing of people confronting a hideous fate.

Meredith Monk started out as a choreographer, but in the 1960s she began presenting works that combine dance, music, and theater. She calls these works "a live movie," "a theater cantata," or "an opera epic," but critics classify them as performance art. In her large-scale "opera" *Quarry*, as the opera opens, Monk lies on a pallet on the floor. She complains she doesn't feel well and falls asleep. The figments of her dreams fill the stage and lead the audience through a maze of dramatic, puzzling, humorous, and poignant experiences.

In September 1994 Monk presented a production on Roosevelt Island, which is situated in the East River in New York City. Roosevelt Island is now mostly a residential community, but its northern and southern ends contain remnants from the nineteenth century. At that time it was known as Welfare Island, and it was home to prisons, poorhouses, hospitals for people with infectious diseases, and asylums.

The first half of the presentation took place late in the afternoon in Lighthouse Park on the northern end of the island. The park was named for a small lighthouse on the grounds, which is said to have been constructed by a madhouse inmate. Spectators sat on a slope and watched as pedestrians strolled, children danced around a tree, people rolled along in wheelchairs, joggers jogged, and a horse with a rider galloped by. At the end of the first half, Monk, dressed in white, sang from the top of the lighthouse. Her amplified voice reached out over the space almost as if the beams of the lighthouse had magically been transformed into music.

The second half, which started an hour later when it was dark, centered around the ruin of a building that used to be a smallpox hospital. The audience sat on bleachers. The cast included plodding convicts, people huddled around a bonfire, pompous doctors, and pitiful patients. In the finale the cast crossed the space in a procession that included a giant skeleton. Monk dressed in black faced into the darkness. The presentation seemed to be ending on a bleak note with images of disease and death. Then light glowed on a hill and the horse stood on the crest like a symbol of hope.

Both Laurie Anderson and Meredith Monk appear at venerated institutions such as the Brooklyn Academy of Music, evidence that a onetime avant-garde medium now holds an accepted place in our culture.

## How to Get Started in Performance Art

For anyone with imagination and who is intrigued by the idea of combining the visual arts, the traditional performing arts, and technological wizardry in new ways, performance art offers limitless opportunities. Many art students go from art school directly into performance art.

The first step toward putting on a performance piece for which you want to be paid would be to interest an organization or individual in contracting for your services. Likely prospects would include museums that want to attract attention to a special exhibit; businesses that are just opening or want to promote a special sale; the owners of new office buildings, housing developments, or retirement communities; or perhaps candidates running for political offices. You no doubt can think of other occasions where performance art can be utilized. You could send a mailing to likely prospects, distribute flyers, or advertise in publications.

If you choose to be an artist who specializes in performance art, you will be embarking on a career that will furnish amusement or edification to others and allow you to use your creative energies in a satisfying way.

# 16

---

# PHOTOGRAPHY

THE ART OF photography is tremendously versatile. Some photographs are valued as great works of art. Other photographs record a world or time apart from our own. Still others function either to illustrate a story, enhance scientific research, or "freeze" an action that is too fast for the human eye to see. The creativity involved in producing photographs is only as limited as one's imagination.

## History of Photography

The photographic process evolved from a search for an aid to drawing. The word *photography* comes from two Greek words meaning to "draw by light." During the Renaissance someone discovered that light entering a small hole in a wall of a dark room throws an inverted image of the scene outside onto the opposite wall. The scene outside could thus be traced on a paper attached to the wall where the image fell. Its discoverers called this arrangement a *camera obscura*, which in Latin means "dark room."

Through the years the camera obscura changed. A lens was put in the hole. A lens forms an image by focusing rays of light, so the use of a lens made the image brighter. The size of the camera obscura gradually became smaller. Then the windows of a sedan chair (an enclosed chair borne on poles by two carriers), were covered, so it could be used as a portable camera obscura. Finally the camera obscura shrank to a box with ground glass for a portion of its top. The image that entered the box through the lens on one side fell on a mirror that was placed at a forty-five degree angle within the box. The mirror reflected the image onto the glass on top of the box. One could trace the image on transparent paper placed over the glass. Today's conventional cameras work on the principle of the camera obscura. In contrast, digital cameras, one of the most popular of today's technological breakthroughs in electronics, no longer depend on chemical or mechanical processes. They all have built-in computers and record images in an entirely electronic form.

## What Photographers Do

With a viewfinder camera the photographer looks through a small peephole that gives an image approximating what a picture snapped at that time would look like. Some viewfinder cameras make adjustments automatically. They thus require fewer decisions on the part of the photographer than other kinds of cameras, but they also offer less control over the outcome.

A single-lens reflex camera permits the photographer to see an image virtually identical to that produced on the film. Because the photographer sees exactly which portions of the photograph will be sharp and which out of focus, this feature aids in composing and focusing. Both the viewfinder camera and the single-lens reflex camera prove ideal for candid photography.

The viewfinder of the twin-lens reflex camera is located on the camera's upper surface. This feature makes it easier to compose a photograph than with a camera held up to the eye. Having the viewfinder on the upper surface also makes it easier to take pictures at or near ground level, say of small children, small animals, or a tiny wildflower, The twin-lens reflex camera uses larger film than the viewfinder camera or the single-lens reflex camera and hence produces larger negatives.

A view camera's sides look like the collapsible part of an accordion. Its disadvantage lies in its large size, which makes it cumbersome to carry and a tripod necessary. A view camera excels for studio work, however, and also for architectural photography. The image on the viewing screen gives an exact image of the negative, enabling a photographer to plan a picture carefully. The image appears upside down, but photographers get used to this. The large film gives good detail.

Polaroid cameras allow a photographer to get immediate results. The renowned photographer Marie Cosindas uses a Polaroid. Her photographs—portraits and still lifes—look like paintings. Ansel Adams, who is well known particularly for his photographs of nature, also used a Polaroid at times.

Digital cameras do not require film. You are immediately able to see how the photograph you are planning to take will look, as a screen built into the camera serves both as the viewfinder and a photo album. If you don't like a picture you have taken, you can delete it from the camera's memory and reuse that space.

The images made with a digital camera that you decide to keep are stored in the camera's memory or in a matchbook-size add-in whose memory is 150 times that of the original IBM computer. You can plug the camera into a computer, transfer the images to a disk for storage, and thus have them available for displaying on the computer screen. If you want, the photographs can be relayed to a TV screen. You can even send images from your computer by e-mail.

Photography prints can be made from the digital photographs in your computer file by a photo shop that has the necessary equipment, or you can make them yourself. With a computer and the proper software, you can alter a digital image in innumerable ways. For instance, you can paint in new textures and backgrounds, substitute colors, change the size of any element in the photo, sharpen images or soften them, add artistic effects such as giving the image an impressionistic look or making it appear as if it were viewed through smoked glass, and more.

The quality of photographs made with a digital camera varies with the cost of the camera. Some authorities say that the most expensive digital cameras make possible photographs whose quality exceeds that of conventional film photography. They believe that today's digital technology is revolutionizing the profession of photography. Others contend that for fine art photography, film is still the best.

Some cameras permit the use of interchangeable lenses. Lenses come in different types to do different jobs—for general use, to give a wide view, or to magnify distant objects. A photographer doesn't need a lot of equipment, however. Henri Cartier-Bresson, the noted French photographer, used only one lens.

Photographers who wish their photographs to qualify as art usually plan carefully before ever taking a photograph. They consider whether the arrangement of the components make an attractive composition. Some take close-ups of commonplace subjects such as a section of a rocky cliff, weathered boards, or a broken window, whose photographic image pleases for the design apparent in it. Some take photographs from unconventional angles or with exaggerated shadows. Some use a high-speed camera to catch images too fleeting for the eye to see. Some use a soft-focus lens, take pictures slightly out of focus, or put a cheesecloth or screen over the lens to secure an impressionistic quality. Photographers use a filter or filters in various combinations over the lens to modify the color or for special effects. They sprinkle water on a lens to make the subject look as if it were viewed through a window with raindrops clinging to it. They use strobe light to bleed out contrasts and intensify blacks and whites. They soften the surface of a Polaroid print chemically and then distort the image with a finger or stick. Artist-photographers use countless means to get the effects they want.

Many artist-photographers take only black-and-white photographs. They believe color gives photographs a postcard quality and fails to convey mood. Such photographers usually develop their own film. Most photographers, however, send their film to commercial laboratories for processing, especially color film because developing color film requires very expensive equipment.

Photographers may try out different developing times to see which time span gives the best result. Sometimes they manipulate a print while developing it to get a more pleasing result. For instance, to keep a dark area from losing detail, they shield that area for part of the exposure time under the enlarger with a cardboard cut the proper shape so as to stop development in that area. This process is called dodging. To accentuate highlights, they cover all of a picture except areas where further development is wanted, so as to give those areas extra exposure time. This latter process is called burning.

Sometimes photographers crop prints to make them more appealing, or they use parts of several photographs in one print. Sometimes they hand-color a print or combine the photographic process with other printmaking techniques such as lithography or silk screening. Photographers use whatever means occur to them to get an interesting result. For instance, computer software, such as Photoshop, makes it possible to manipulate photographic images without chemicals. Even if you don't use a digital camera, you can digitally scan the photographic prints and then import them into a program that allows you to burn, dodge, accent highlights, crop, and even combine several images into one.

## Using Your Photography Skills

Most early photographs were portraits. For the earliest portraits the process required that the subject refrain from moving for fifteen minutes while the camera did its work. Clamps held the sitter's head still. Improvements soon shortened the exposure time. Photographers often journeyed from town to town, as almost everyone wanted his or her portrait taken. Today, of course, photographers take portraits in their studios or go to the subject's home or some other location that provides a good background. Cameras smaller than the bulky ones of the past make transporting them easy.

Documentary photographers record different aspects of a single subject, such as the sights of a city, a certain type of human activity, the grandeur of the wilderness. Early in the twentieth century, Jean-Eugène Auguste Atget took hundreds of photographs in and around Paris of historic buildings, lowly hovels, fountains, people, and street scenes. The Museum of Modern Art in New York City owns his negatives and periodically exhibits prints made from them.

A documentary photographer often does more than convey information with photographs. In the latter part of the nineteenth century, Jacob Riis photographed the deplorable conditions in the slums of New York City. As a result of his photographs, better housing eventually replaced tenements. In the beginning of the twentieth century, Lewis W. Hine took photographs of children working in factories. His photographs led to laws that prohibit the exploitation of children by industry.

In the 1930s Dorothea Lange used her camera to document the problems of farmers in the Dust Bowl—parts of Texas, New Mexico, Colorado, Kansas, and Oklahoma, where improper farming methods, overgrazing of the land, and dry weather resulted in dust storms that blew away the topsoil. Many people from that area abandoned their land and set out across the country with few possessions and little money, hoping to find a better life elsewhere, particularly in California. Magazines and newspapers published Lange's photographs, making the public aware of the plight of these people and their need for assistance.

A photojournalist takes photographs relating to current news stories and usually works for a newspaper, news magazine, or television station. Sports photography is a specialized kind of photojournalism. To secure a position as a photojournalist with a publication, you would need to assemble a portfolio of photos you have taken of newsworthy subjects to show to a prospective employer. It would be particularly helpful if you had taken photos of a circumstance that had recently taken place.

A fashion photographer takes photographs for fashion magazines, the fashion pages of newspapers, and advertisements for clothing. Those working in fashion photography claim their work often presents a social statement, as it sometimes portrays people in real-life situations: on the job, at home, or taking part in sports or other activities. Art museums sometimes display the fashion photography of noted photographers such as the late Richard Avedon. If you wish to become a fashion photographer, assemble a portfolio of photos you have taken of friends fashionably dressed and posed in appropriate settings to show to prospective employers.

Science makes use of photography, too. The photographs of scientific photographers appear in scientific publications, research reports, and textbooks. A camera fitted with a microscope can take pictures of things too small for the naked eye to see, often revealing curious patterns. A camera fitted to a telescope takes pictures of stars, galaxies, meteors, and whatever else appears in the heavens. Underwater photographers take pictures of creatures and plants that live in the ocean and other bodies of water and sometimes document the remains of submerged shipwrecks that hold untold treasures. Underwater photographers go as deep as one and a half miles below the surface of the ocean in a submersible vessel and from its portholes photograph creatures never before seen by humans. Biomedical photographers take photographs of medical procedures such as surgery. Anyone desiring to be a scientific photographer would seek employment at natural history museums, scientific institutions and publications, and the like.

Commercial photographers take photographs for advertisements, magazines, catalogs, book illustrations, annual reports of corporations, and much more. Some photographers work for local television stations or national or cable networks, covering news events as part of a team. Cinematographers take moving pictures shown in theaters or for educational and other purposes.

Some photographers specialize in aerial photography, which got its impetus from military use after the invention of the airplane. Interpreters study photographs taken from reconnaissance planes to gain military information. Governments also employ aerial photographers to make photographic surveys of cities, coastlines, farmlands, and wilderness areas. Aerial photographers help archaeologists discover prehistoric sites through the use of infrared film, which reveals details indiscernible to the naked eye. Aerial photographers also help geologists find likely spots for the discovery of oil and make it possible for naturalists to count wild animal populations.

To specialize in taking photographs from an airplane or a blimp, you undoubtedly would have to be employed by an organization that wanted such photos.

Another type of photograph that a photographer can specialize in is wedding photographs. If one specializes in wedding photographs, one could take a traditional approach or a photojournalistic or candid approach. Because weddings are usually held on weekends, one could start a career in this field while still holding down a full-time job doing something else so as to be sure of a livelihood. Wedding photography is usually done on a location of the subjects' choosing, so having a studio isn't necessary. The same is true when one photographs parties.

In 2002 the median annual earnings of salaried photographers who worked full-time were about $24,040. The median 50 percent earned between $17,740 and $34,910. The lowest 10 percent earned less than $14,640, while the top 10 percent earned more than $49,920. Median annual earnings of salaried photographers working for newspapers and periodicals were $31,460 and $21,860 respectively. Very few photographers who seek to earn their livelihood solely through producing artistic photographs are successful enough to support themselves. Most such photographers find it necessary to use their photographic skills in other ways to support themselves.

Most everyone is fascinated by good photographs, so if you wish to make photography your means of livelihood and are a good photographer, you will likely find buyers for your pictures. Whatever type of photographs you make, you can be sure that you will have a career rich in possibilities.

# 17

---

# Printmaking

PRINTMAKING IS THOUGHT to have originated in China. As paper-making and printing spread to and flourished throughout Europe, printmaking began to take on the qualities of fine art. By the first half of the twentieth century, prints became immensely popular through the works of artists like Picasso, Miró, Kandinsky, Klee, and others.

## What Printmakers Do

A printmaker creates a picture or other design on one surface and transfers it to another—most often by inking the original design, covering it with a sheet of paper, and applying pressure. By repeating this process, a series of identical prints can be made. All prints of a series rank as original works of art.

Woodcuts or wood prints are probably the oldest kind of print, originating in China and spreading to northern Europe by the end of the fourteenth century. An artist making a woodcut cuts a design into a block of wood. The wood used nowadays is usually high-quality plywood, which makes for easier carving of the image. The artist first draws, paints, or pastes a design on the wood as a guide. With knives, gouges, and chisels, the artist cuts away areas that are to represent blank space in the design, leaving in relief the areas the artist wants printed. The artist achieves texture by scraping, hammering, or scratching the woodblock. Sometimes the grain of the wood serves as part of the design. Woodcuts often display bold lines and large uninked areas.

A print made from a design cut into the end grain of a hardwood block is called a *wood engraving*. The artist uses tools called *gravers* and *burins* to do the cutting. As with a woodcut, the artist leaves in relief the lines and areas to be printed, usually defining the lines more sharply than those of a woodcut.

An artist makes a print from a woodblock by applying a sticky ink to the raised portions with a roller, then pressing a piece of paper against the block either with an implement held in the hand or a press. The paper absorbs the ink, transferring to the paper an impression of the raised portion of the woodblock. When desiring more than one color in a woodcut or wood engraving, the artist cuts a block for each color, cutting away the parts of each block that are not to be printed in that color.

Artists also use materials other than wood for relief printing, for instance, linoleum, cardboard, plaster, or Plexiglas. A print of a design cut into linoleum is called a *linocut*.

An intaglio print is made from a metal plate, usually copper or zinc. The artist cuts or etches the design into the plate. Ink is applied to the plate, and then the surface wiped clean, allowing ink in the incised or etched lines and areas to remain. Consequently, in the printing process these incised or etched lines and areas are printed rather than raised lines and areas, as is the case in relief printing. Using a metal plate makes possible thinner lines than those obtained with a woodcut; thus delicacy, complexity, and richness of texture often characterize intaglio prints.

An engraving is one type of intaglio print. An artist who wishes to make an engraving uses gravers and burins to cut the design into a metal plate and then wipes away the burr (a thin ridge of metal that is thrown up on either side of the cuts).

Another type of intaglio print is the drypoint print. An artist who wishes to make a drypoint print uses a needle with a steel or diamond tip to cut the design into a metal plate. Such a needle gives the artist almost as much freedom as drawing on paper affords. Typically the depth of a groove made in this way is slight. More effort produces heavier lines, but they usually appear less freely moving. The needle throws up a burr on either side of the groove. The burrs are allowed to remain in place. After inking, both the grooves and the buffs hold ink. As a result, the ink line transferred to the paper assumes a soft velvety appearance. Because of the burr's fragility, an artist finds it impossible to make more than a small number of prints from a drypoint plate unless a thin coating of steel added by an electrolytic process protects the burrs. One can apply such a coating only if the plate is copper.

Etchings are also intaglio prints. An artist who wishes to make an etching first coats a metal plate with etching ground, which may be either wax or a tarlike substance. When the etching ground dries, the artist cuts a design into the etching ground with needles and other tools, thereby exposing the metal. The artist then immerses the plate in an acid bath. Etching ground is acid-resistant, so the acid etches only the exposed metal. The artist removes the plate from the acid bath after the acid etches the metal to the depth wished for the finest lines in the composition. The artist then covers these lines with a stop-out varnish and returns the plate to the acid bath. The stop-out varnish prevents the acid from acting further on the lines it covers. When other lines reach the depth wished for them, the artist applies stop-out varnish to them and returns the plate to the acid bath. The artist repeats this process (called *biting*) as many times as desired. This procedure makes possible a wide tonal range.

After the completion of the process, the artist removes the etching ground from the plate with a solvent. Etched lines look rougher than lines in an engraving and consequently appear similar to drawing. The tonal range in etchings allows shading darker and richer than the shading in other print mediums herein discussed. One sees these characteristics in the etchings of Rembrandt, the supreme master of the etching technique.

An aquatint is a kind of etching. To make an aquatint, an artist either drips melted powdered rosin onto a metal plate or sprays enamel on it. The artist cuts a design into the surface thus obtained and immerses the plate in an acid bath. As rosin and enamel are acid-resistant, the acid doesn't affect areas covered by them. As with a regular etching, the artist probably exposes some parts of the plate to the acid longer than others. The aquatint process enables an artist to obtain tones from silvery to a rich black similar to those of watercolor washes—hence the name aquatint. *Aqua*, of course, is the Latin word for water.

A mezzotint also is made with a metal plate, but in this case the ink prints the background rather than the design. The artist pits the surface of the plate with a device called a *rocker*. The pitted surface prints a solid, velvety black, so the artist can scrape away at the pitted surface where he or she wants lighter tones in the print. The scraped surfaces hold less ink than the pitted background and so print a lighter tone. The artist polishes the plate where white areas are desired, as a polished surface will not hold ink. *Mezzo* means half in Italian; the mezzotint process gets its name from the fact that the process makes halftones possible.

To give color to an intaglio print, an artist wipes different colored inks onto different areas of the plate or prepares a separate plate for each color. If more than one plate is prepared for this purpose, the plates are printed in succession. Additional colors desired for small areas can be hand painted.

When making a print from a metal plate, the artist applies the ink and then wipes it off with a muslin called *tarlatan*, usually allowing ink to remain only in the grooves. Sometimes, however, an artist leaves a pale haze of ink on the other portions of the print so as to secure a slight tone in those areas. The artist places the plate on a press, covers it with dampened paper, then with layers of wool printing felt. Rollers apply pressure to the assemblage, forcing the paper and felt into the grooves in the plate, thus bringing the paper into contact with the ink. In this way, the image cut into the plate transfers to the paper in reverse.

An artist makes a plate for a collograph by gluing pieces of fabric, paper, string, or other materials to a backing. Impressing a collograph plate without using ink results in an embossment.

Lithography is another method of creating prints. Lithography can reproduce subtle nuances, say of flesh tone or hair texture. Traditionally an artist who created lithographs drew or painted the desired image with a greasy pencil, crayon, or tusche (a black liquid) on a limestone block leveled and given a fine finish. A fine-grained marble slab also could be used. Nowadays, however, a zinc or aluminum plate is more commonly used.

For a lithographic print with more than one color, the artist prepares a separate stone or metal plate for each color. Sometimes a master printer takes over at this point, though the artist may do the printing as well as preparing the stone or plate. Whoever does the printing applies various mixtures to the surface of the stone or plate to make the open areas insensitive to ink and the greasy images water repellent and receptive to ink. Then the printer dampens the stone or plate and applies ink with a roller. The ink adheres to the greasy images but not to the other areas.

A sheet of paper is placed on the stone or plate and a lubricated paper or cloth called a *tympan* is placed over the first paper. Pressure applied to this assemblage causes the ink to transfer to the paper in contact with it. If the artist prepared more than one stone or plate—one for each color—they are used successively.

Stencils provide a way of making a type of print called a *screen print*, *silk-screen print*, or *serigraph*. To make a stencil, an artist stretches a fine mesh material, usually nylon or metal rather than silk, across a frame, thus producing a screen. From this point, the procedure varies.

In one method, the artist draws a design on paper or on a lacquer film supported by a backing and then cuts away the areas that are not to be printed.

In another method, the artist prepares a stencil by drawing on the screen with grease pencils or with a brush and tusche, covering the screen with glue, and then removing the drawing with a solvent, leaving a glue stencil.

Artists also make stencils by drawing a design with an opaque material on a transparent plastic sheet, placing the sheet in contact with a sensitive emulsion and exposing it to light. The emulsion hardens in areas where the light passes through but remains soft in areas covered by the drawing material. After the emulsion hardens in the desired areas, the artist washes away the soft emulsion and drawing material, thus opening the image.

To print from a stencil, the artist hinges the frame with the screen stretched over it to a board, so that the stencil can be brought in contact with a piece of paper laid on the board. The artist presses ink (liquid enough to pass through the screen but not so liquid that it runs) through the screen onto the paper with a squeegee. The impenetrable parts of the stencil prevent ink from reaching areas beneath them. To produce a print with more than one color, the artist makes a stencil for each color.

Artists also screen print on silk, wool, cotton, burlap, and suede, employing matte and metallic inks. Screen-printed fabrics make attractive bedspreads, curtains, wall hangings, upholstery material, carpets, banners, and clothing.

## Limited Edition Prints

Usually an artist pulls only a limited number of prints from one design and numbers them. After pulling the desired number, the artist most often destroys a woodblock from which woodcuts or wood engravings were made, the metal plate from which intaglio prints were made, or the stencils from which screen prints were made; or, he or she marks them in such a way that further prints made from them would be disfigured, an action called *striking*. Lithographic stones are ground down after pulling the desired number of prints, thus making it possible to use the stones again. The artist takes these actions to prevent further prints from being made; a large number of identical prints in existence lessens the value of a print.

A monotype is a print made by a method that generally yields between one or possibly two or three good impressions of the image the artist has prepared on a nonabsorbent surface such as smooth metal, smooth stone, a plastic sheet, glass, or Plexiglas. The artist creates the desired image on the surface of one of these materials with printing inks, oil paints, or any other slow drying medium, or the artist may cover the entire surface with one of these mediums, either with a brush or by rolling it on, and then wipe away the areas that are to remain light.

Once the plate is prepared, the artist presses a sheet of absorbent paper against the image by hand or by using an etching press or even a laundry wringer. This action creates an image on the paper. It is impossible to make more than up to three satisfactory prints of the image, as the medium with which the image was made dissipates beyond printability.

Sometimes an artist reworks the "ghost" image left on the plate after pulling monotypes, either by manipulating the material on the plate and/or adding more of the material that was used to make the original image. The artist can then make further prints somewhat like but different from the first ones.

A printmaker chooses the paper for an edition of prints with care, as the texture and color of the paper contribute to the final effect. The paper must be strong, particularly if the process involves pressure. Also the paper must absorb ink satisfactorily so as to produce subtle variations of tone and line. Artists value rag papers over other types. Dealers import handsome papers from Europe and the Orient, and some papermakers in the United States produce desirable papers. Sometimes a printmaker makes the paper rather than buying it.

## New Methods in Printmaking

In the past, artists produced mostly small prints in only one color and with delicate lines (except for the bold lines of woodcuts). Today prints come as large as four feet by twelve feet, bold designs predominate, and multicolored prints find many purchasers. Following the lead of painters, printmakers sometimes make prints in irregular shapes, rather than the rectangular shape adhered to in the past.

Some artists combine different ways of printmaking. Artists have long produced combinations of engraving, etching, drypoint, mezzotint, and aquatint. Today they not only combine traditional techniques but also try new ways of making prints. For example, they sometimes press textured materials into a soft etching ground to achieve unusual effects. They may also combine photographic processes with other printmaking processes. Or, they may create three-dimensional sculptures by cutting and folding printed papers or by assembling precut printed surfaces. Artists use any way of making a print that their imaginations suggest.

If your prints are appealing, you can be sure there are people who would like to have them hanging in their homes or offices, and you would have the satisfaction of pursuing a worthwhile career.

# 18

# Quilt Making

Quilts typically are used to cover a bed. However, sometimes the artistry involved in making a quilt and the beautiful decorations that adorn it elevate it to a place on the wall, where many can admire and appreciate it.

## History of Quilt Making

The tradition of quilt making in America goes back to pioneer days. When settlers first came to this country, cloth was scarce. Consequently, housewives made good use of every scrap of fabric that came their way. When adult clothing became worn, mothers used the parts still in good condition to make children's clothing. When children's clothing wore out, any salvageable fabric in all likelihood got cut into pieces and sewn into a quilt, which helped provide warmth at night.

The most admired quilts are those made by the Amish, a religious sect that settled mostly in Pennsylvania and Ohio. The Amish women used store-bought, uniformly colored wool to create America's first major abstract art. Museums and collectors treasure their creations.

Quilt making not only served a useful purpose, it also provided an outlet for artistic instincts. In early times, a woman's day was filled with seemingly endless chores. Quilt making gave a respite from drudgery and an opportunity to create beauty. In making quilts, these women created a legacy, something tangible and worthwhile to hand down to future generations.

Today quilts still offer an opportunity for artistic expression and are appreciated for their beauty. In recent years the appreciation of quilts has increased tremendously. Frequently they hang on walls as decorative items, or they may serve as bedspreads.

## What Quilt Makers Do

Anyone wishing to make a quilt must first decide upon a pattern. Many quilt patterns from the past are still used. They have names such as Double Wedding Ring (the most popular quilt pattern of all time), Double Irish Chain, Dresden Plate, Birds in Air, Drunkard's Path, Flower Garden, School House, Log Cabin, and Orange Peel. Representations of these and instructions for making them can be found in books available in craft stores and libraries.

In the early twentieth century, women's magazines and newspaper sewing columns began making quilt patterns available by mail order. New patterns influenced by the Arts and Crafts movement and later the art deco style were devised. Modern quilt makers sometimes invent new patterns and choose fabrics that reflect the quilt maker's individuality.

Designs can be worked out on graph paper. After the pattern and the fabrics are decided upon, the next step is cutting the desired shapes from the fabrics to be used.

A quilt maker can make a quilt top by piecing, which means sewing pieces of cloth together. Piecing is also called *patchwork.* Nowadays rather than using scraps of fabric cut from discarded clothing or left over from other sewing projects, a quilt maker usually buys new fabric, cuts it into pieces the proper sizes (usually geometric shapes), and sews them together to create a quilt top in the desired pattern. Sometimes a quilt maker prepares pieced squares all the same size and sews them together to make a quilt top with a pattern in all squares the same, two patterns alternating, or with different patterns in each square. In other pieced quilts, a single design covers the entire top. Cutting fabric into pieces and then sewing them together sounds foolish, but works of art result.

Appliqué provides another way of giving pattern to a quilt top. For an appliquéd quilt, rather than sewing pieces of fabric together to make a top, the quilt maker sews the pieces that make the pattern on top of a fabric the size the finished quilt is to be. If desired, cotton stuffed between the appliquéd pieces and the background gives a three-dimensional effect.

One way of inserting stuffing under appliquéd designs is called *trapunto.* In this method, one bastes a muslin backing to the quilt top, marks the quilting design on the muslin, and stitches the outlines of the design from the reverse side. Slits are then made on the reverse side of areas where stuffing is desired and cotton is stuffed into these areas. The slits are then sewed up. This technique works very well with a quilt top comprised of a single piece of cloth.

An appliquéd quilt top is sometimes constructed of squares sewn together. Appliquéd quilts don't require geometric shapes, so they sometimes portray a scene, for example, a farmyard or a woodland view or a bouquet of flowers. Embroidered accents can add further embellishment.

In the nineteenth century, native Hawaiian quilt makers developed a technique of making appliquéd quilts with a lacy look. The principle is the same as that demonstrated when a child folds a paper once or several times, cuts a pattern through the folded paper, then opens the paper, revealing a balanced design. To make such a pattern, a quilt maker experiments with paper cutouts on a small scale, then he or she prepares a paper pattern of the final design in the desired scale. Using the paper pattern as a guide, the quilt maker traces the pattern onto the fabric that is to be appliquéd onto a background fabric, cuts out the areas where the background material is to show through, and then appliqués the cutout fabric to the background. A quilt top also can be a single piece of material with an embroidered design.

After completing a quilt top, the quilt maker bastes together the top, an inner lining, and the material that is to serve as the underside and stitches through the three layers in a manner that results in the stitching making an attractive pattern. The stitching usually follows the contours of the design. For decorative stitching in background areas, freehand drawing or drawings made with the aid of a template can serve as a guide. A template is a cardboard pattern the quilt maker devises. In either case, the quilt maker decides on a design appropriate for the space available. This stitching is called *quilting*.

Traditionally quilters quilted by hand; today they sometimes use a sewing machine. A quilter who quilts by hand takes pride in small, even stitches. Sometimes the quilting is delegated to others, say to members of a church group who take on quilting projects as a means of earning money for their church.

Before beginning the quilting, quilters usually stretch the quilt horizontally on a frame that holds the material taut. Several people can stitch at the same time on a quilt held in a frame. Such gatherings are called *quilting bees*. Quilting bees give women an opportunity to socialize. Frontier women often lived far from each other, and in later times women were still pretty much confined to their homes, so quilting bees provided an opportunity to socialize.

When making a so-called crazy quilt, one sews pieces of fabric of varying shapes with embroidery stitches to a muslin backing, completely covering the muslin and sometimes embroidering ornamental motifs on individual pieces. The end result is a charming hodgepodge. In Victorian times, a person making a crazy quilt used mostly pieces of velvet, silk, ribbon, and printed fabrics. Consequently, Victorian crazy quilts present an opulent look. A modern quilt maker could fashion a crazy quilt to rival those of the past.

After finishing a crazy-quilt top, the maker attaches batting and backing to it by tufting. Tufting means threading through layers of cloth and perhaps batting and back again and then tying the thread ends (probably yarn) to create a tuft, usually at regular intervals. In the case of a crazy quilt, the thread goes only through the back and the batting, not through the top.

Modern quilt makers sometimes paint, crayon, or dye a design on a quilt top or use photographic means to transfer an image. The materials used in making the transfer can be selected so that the quilt will withstand washing.

Fashion designers sometimes use quilted materials in their creations. Most often their quilted garments flaunt bright colors and trapunto. Individual seamstresses follow their lead and produce handmade, one-of-a-kind articles of quilted wearing apparel.

Quilt making has given pleasure to generations of women and sometimes to men as well. It continues to give pleasure today and can be not only an immensely satisfying undertaking, but a profitable one as well.

# 19

# SCULPTURE

SCULPTORS ARE ARTISTS who work in three dimensions. They fashion works of art out of almost any material: stone, wood, metal, clay, plaster, cement, plastic, paper pulp, glass, fabric, even baker's dough. Sculptures range from anything so small one could balance it on the end of a finger to very large. Sculptures may classify as realistic, stylized, abstract, or nonrepresentational and may be in the round or in relief. The latter term applies to images that project from a more or less flat surface.

## History of Sculpture

Evidence reaching back into prehistoric times affirms the inclination of human beings to create sculptural images. As many as forty thousand years ago, people of the Ice Age modeled sculptures of clay and also carved them from stone, mammoth ivory, reindeer antlers, and bone. Figures of women and animals sculpted in these materials and dating from that era periodically come to light in caves and elsewhere throughout Europe.

Ancient Greek sculptures of bronze and stone also have survived, including unfinished ones of stone that tell us something of the Greek sculptor's way of working with that material. The artist drew an outline of a figure on the block and then chipped away excess stone from all sides, releasing the form that early Greeks believed was imprisoned in the block.

Sculptures contribute a great deal to the beauty of Gothic cathedrals built in Europe in the Middle Ages. Most people at that time did not know how to read, so the clergy used sculptures as well as stained glass windows, mosaics, and paintings to acquaint the populace with the contents of the Bible. When a town and its clergy decided to build a cathedral, the clergy conferred with a master builder or architect, who in turn relayed instructions to stonemasons. The amount of sculptural work in a cathedral is immense and sometimes took hundreds of years to complete.

## What Sculptors Do

After making a drawing or drawings of the work he or she intends to create, a sculptor may model one or more small figures in clay, wax, or plaster as an aid to determining what the finished work should look like.

A beginner may find using plasticine, a prepared modeling clay that requires no preparation and almost no inner supports, the best material for creating a model. Plasticine can be purchased at art supply stores, as can modeling tools. Desirable tools are blade-shaped ones—one with a single wire end and another with two wire ends. A smooth board that has been given a couple coats of shellac makes a good base for modeling. One also can model on a table with a nonporous top (say a porcelain-topped kitchen table or one covered with oilcloth). The plasticine is cut up and kneaded into shapes about the size of a banana. These shapes are piled on the table. The sculptor then washes his or her hands and is ready to begin.

When planning a stone sculpture, after deciding on its form, the sculptor might make an enlargement in clay (or whatever material is used for preliminary models) the size of the intended work before beginning work on the stone block. If the sculptor plans to cast the sculpture in metal, an enlargement in clay or other material in the size intended for the final work is a necessity.

When making a stone sculpture, measurements from a full-sized model can be transferred to the block of stone with a mechanical device called a *pointing machine*, which is available at art supply stores. For a work larger than the model, the measurements on the stone block necessarily have to be increased proportionately. The pointing machine indicates where holes in the stone should be drilled to correspond to strategic points on the model. The holes act as guides in the carving. Using a pointing machine makes possible the creation of complicated works that would be impossible to execute otherwise.

Michelangelo created his marble sculptures by direct carving rather than using a pointing machine. He began work on a sculpture that was to be in the round as if carving a relief. That is, he worked from the front toward the back, creating figures astonishingly lifelike. Assistants helped him, but only under the closest supervision.

Some sculptors whose finished works are of stone, after creating the model, turn the rest of the process over to assistants. They consider conceiving the idea and constructing the model the creative parts of the process. Assistants transfer the measurements to the stone block and do the carving and any final filing and polishing. Auguste Rodin, the famous French sculptor of the late nineteenth and early twentieth centuries whom critics consider the greatest sculptor since Michelangelo, mostly depended on his assistants to translate his models of clay, plaster, and wax into stone or bronze.

The Englishman Henry Moore, the most outstanding sculptor since Rodin, carved stone and wood directly without mechanical aids. He worked round and round his stone and wood sculptures rather than from front to back, producing simple, bold, and monumental works. Barbara Hepworth, also an English sculptor, likewise believed in the direct approach when working with stone or wood. Moore's and Hepworth's method of making sculptures of stone and wood corresponds to that of ancient Greek sculptors.

Wood carving probably predated stone carving. Few wood carvings from antiquity survive, however, because of wood's susceptibility to the ravages of weather, insects, and fungi. Because of its vulnerability, wood proves more suitable for carvings that will be kept inside rather than outdoors. Some medieval statues of saints carved in wood do survive, and fabulous centuries-old carved wood altarpieces still grace the interiors of cathedrals and churches in southern Germany and Austria.

Wood, being softer than stone, is, of course, easier to carve than stone. Also wood contrasts with stone in that wood imparts a feeling of warmth while stone conveys a feeling of coldness. The grain of wood also adds to wood's appeal. The size of the tree from which a block of wood comes naturally limits the size of the block. As a result, wood carvings tend to be in human scale or smaller, rather than in the heroic proportions of some stone sculptures. For a larger work made from wood, one can join pieces of wood.

A carver in wood proceeds much as does the carver in stone. Sometimes the shape of a block of wood itself suggests a subject. Probably the woodcarver first sketches on paper to develop an idea and then uses clay or some other easily worked material to make a three-dimensional interpretation of the sketch. After the sculptor determines the form of the wood carving, he or she may draw front, rear, and side views of the design on the block. Once the carving is underway, the drawing soon disappears, of course, but it serves as a guide in the beginning. When making a sizable sculpture, sculptors who carve wood today probably cut away most of the excess wood with a power saw and then finish the carving with mallet and chisels, rasps, rifflers, and scrapers. Tool marks left on the surface of the wood can give an interesting texture, or the sculptor may smooth the surface.

Sculptors sometimes partly or completely paint their wood sculptures. In this they follow the example of predecessors, for remnants of paint on ancient Greek stone sculptures tell us that they were originally painted at least partially, particularly the hair, eyes, and clothing. We know that medieval sculptors painted both wood and stone sculptures. Early Roman and Renaissance artists didn't paint white marble sculptures but did paint sculptures of other materials. Because paint protects, the paint on ancient wood sculptures undoubtedly helped those still in existence to survive. Painted sculptures need to be repainted about every seven years.

Sculptors who make sculptures of metal make them of bronze, brass, aluminum, tin, lead, silver, or gold. Through the centuries bronze, an alloy of copper and tin and sometimes small amounts of other metals, has been the favored material for metal sculpture.

Bronze and other metal sculptures are cast, a process that allows more freedom in designing than does carving as it permits greater detail and larger dimensions. The artist creates a full-scale model in clay, wax, or other easily formed material and then most often entrusts the casting to a foundry. The foundry uses either the sand-casting method or the lost-wax method to make a metal image of the full-scale model. When the casting process is completed, foundry workers or the sculptor chisel away seams and correct faults. Sometimes they apply chemicals to bronze surfaces to give them a colored patina.

Ruth Asawa, a Japanese-American artist, created a bronze fountain to serve as the centerpiece of the approach to a hotel in downtown San Francisco. Using baker's dough, she first sculpted a circular form like the surround of a well and then applied small figures and scenes that are representative of San Francisco to it. A mold of her creation was made, from which the fountain was cast in bronze. The fountain gives pleasure not only by the upward thrust and downward splash of its water jet but also by the images on its base, which delight all who take the time to look at them.

A relief sculpture can be made by hammering and pressing a design into sheet metal, a process called *chasing*. When done from the reverse side, the process is called *repoussé*. The sheet metal may be placed over a mold that serves as a guide. Workers shaped the three-hundred copper sheets that form the Statue of Liberty by the repoussé method. A framework of steel supports the copper sheets.

Modern sculptors sometimes use welding and forging techniques to make metal sculptures. These techniques make possible constructions of materials such as sheet metal, wire, and metal rods and tubes. The resulting sculptures emphasize flat planes and line. The Spanish sculptor Julio Gonzales, who made such sculptures, called them "drawings in space," as they are mostly linear rather than three-dimensional. In this kind of sculpture particularly, the negative spaces—that is, the openings in it—often play as important a role as the solid parts.

Alexander Calder fashioned objects he called *mobiles* and *stabiles* from metal sheeting, rods, and wires. Mobiles hang in space so that air currents set their parts in motion. Stabiles sit on the ground or a floor. Timothy Rose of Sausalito, California, apparently was inspired by Calder, as he produces colorful, whimsical mobiles crafted of sheet metal, wire, plywood, and acrylic paint. He prices his mobiles from $100 to $400.

Some artists make sculptural constructions out of so-called found objects, such as automobile and engine parts, tools, furniture components, anything at all. John Chamberlain used crushed automobile parts to create sculptures. Picasso fastened a bicycle's handlebars and seat together in a way that suggests a bull's head with horns. Such sculptures are called *assemblages*.

Clay sculptures not only serve as preliminary models for sculptures in other materials but may be art objects in their own right. The properties of clay enable it to be easily manipulated when moist; when fired, it becomes hard.

The sculptor in clay usually first draws sketches of possible subjects. After choosing one as a model, he or she kneads the clay to an even texture and then prepares rolls of clay. For a small sculpture, say a foot high or less, the artist forms the basic shape with the rolls of clay, presses pellets of clay onto the basic shape to fill it out and add details, and then textures or smooths the surface or leaves it as it is.

A clay sculpture over a foot high requires an armature, an inner support of metal pipe and/or wire to prevent the sculpture from collapsing before being fired. If an artist does not finish a clay sculpture in one session, he or she covers it with a damp cloth or cloths to keep the clay moist, so that clay added later will adhere.

Clay contracts somewhat while drying, so the artist keeps all thicknesses approximately equal to ensure that they contract evenly. A clay sculpture must dry completely before firing. Firing takes place in a kiln, a kind of oven. Firing makes clay about as hard as stone. If the sculptor doesn't own a kiln, a nearby ceramist or the ceramics department of a school may undertake this part of the process.

Fingers can be used for sculpting clay as well as wooden blades and tools with wire ends. An artist gives color to a clay object by applying glaze (a glassy coating), slip (a thin mixture of clay and water), or paint.

Artists also use supple materials like fabric, vinyl, or foam rubber to make sculptures. Forms devised of soft material filled with stuffing hang on walls, suspend from ceilings, or sit wherever you want. Sometimes artists paint portions of a soft sculpture or attach things to it. Gerhardt Knodel hung narrow strips of cloth from an arching framework of thin wire for an ethereal three-dimensional composition. Piero Gilardi created life-size "landscapes" of colored foam rubber that roll up for transporting. One of his landscapes features a "cobblestone street," another a "vegetable garden"—all of colored foam rubber. Often soft sculptures are whimsical, like Claes Oldenburg's giant hamburger of sailcloth.

The materials artists use for sculptures seem limitless. Artists blow glass into sculptures and cast sculptures of glass, paper pulp, plastics such as acrylic and polyester, and cement with dry color and stone dust added for sparkle. Almost any material you can think of can be utilized to make sculptures.

Sculptors of other eras surely never dreamed of some of the types of sculptures created nowadays. Many sculptures today are nonobjective rather than representing anything in the real world. Sometimes parts move, powered by air currents, electromechanical means, water, magnetism, or the spectator. Sometimes sculptures incorporate flashing lights or flowing water controlled by computer. Some artists bend neon tubes into sculpture. Others engineer sculptural earthworks out-of-doors and also in galleries and museums. Some of these so-called environmental sculptures reach monumental proportions—for instance, Robert Smithson's *Spiral Jetty*, a fifteen-hundred-foot-long construction of rock, basalt, and earth at a remote site on the Great Salt Lake in Utah.

George Segal enlists real people to serve as models for his usually white, rough plaster casts that he presents as finished sculptures. He also creates elegant bronze figures. Segal places his figures in common situations like lounging around at a costume party or waiting for a bus. People at the New York City Port Authority's bus terminal take snapshots of friends standing in line behind Segal's patiently waiting figures.

The late Ed Kienholz also made life-size figures, but of resin. He arranged his figures in environments of real objects or junk constructions. In his *Beanery*, a representation of a hangout in Los Angeles, his people wear real clothes, but clocks substitute for their heads. All the clocks show the same time—ten after ten.

To get an idea for a sculpture, solve the problems involved, and bring the work to a satisfying conclusion represents a significant accomplishment requiring both intellectual and physical prowess. An artist who brings off such a feat deserves the highest praise.

Sometimes organizations, governmental or otherwise, commission a sculptor to create a sculpture for a specific location. Some cities require that designers of public projects and the builders of large buildings allocate a certain percentage of their budgets for art. The art commissioned for such sites most often is sculpture.

If a sculptor's creations are intriguing, success will surely come.

# 20

---

# STAINED GLASS

CREATING A STAINED glass object or window is an old and exacting art. The artists who produced them in the past as well as those practitioners of the art today are highly creative and possess excellent technical abilities.

## History of Stained Glass

No one knows when someone first used stained glass for windows. Latin texts of the third and fourth centuries A.D. mention colored-glass windows in early Christian churches. The earliest material evidence—pieces of green, blue, amber, and red glass—came from the site of a late seventh-century abbey in England. The cut of some of the glass edges makes it apparent the glass came from windows.

The most glorious stained glass windows from previous centuries still in existence ornament Gothic cathedrals built in Europe in the twelfth and thirteenth centuries. These windows fill vast areas with variously colored glass set between vertical supports of wood and stone. A square yard of window sometimes contains as many as four hundred pieces of colored glass.

Taking a blob of molten glass on the end of a blowpipe, a glassblower blew it into a cylindrical shape. He cut the ends off the cylinder, split it lengthwise, and lay the halves on a stone. The halves flattened and solidified, forming sheets of irregular thickness. This irregularity in thickness contributes to the charm of ancient glass, as do the streaks, ripples, and bubbles in it. Through the centuries, weather pitted the glass and dust collected in the depressions so formed. Shadings resulted, further enhancing the beauty of the glass.

In the early fourteenth century, artists began to use enamel to paint inscriptions and details such as facial features and drapery folds on stained glass windows. After painting the glass, they fired it in a kiln to fuse the enamel to the glass. Later artists painted scenes and figures on glass windows. They used clear glass or glass of subdued color to enable their paintings to show to the best advantage. This practice resulted in windows that lacked the vibrant color of earlier stained glass windows.

Originally the lead strips that held the components of a stained glass window in place served as part of the design and added to its attractiveness. When painting on glass became popular, artists avoided using lead strips if possible. New glassmaking techniques produced smoother, thinner glass lacking the vitality of the older glass. These changes also lessened the beauty of the windows. In time the process that created the magnificent windows of the twelfth and thirteenth centuries became a lost art.

The nineteenth century brought a renewed interest in Gothic architecture. Architects undertook the job of renovating the great Gothic cathedrals. As an aid to this endeavor, Violett-le-Duc, the French Minister of Public Monuments at the time, researched the methods of Gothic construction and, in so doing, he rediscovered the old ways of making stained glass windows. A renaissance in the use of stained glass began. Pale or colorless glass with paintings on them gave way to richly colored glass areas separated by lead.

In the late nineteenth century and on into the twentieth century, Louis Comfort Tiffany, the son of a dealer in jewelry, silver, and art objects in New York City, did much to revitalize the art of stained glass in the United States. Fortunately Tiffany possessed the resources to pursue his interests fully. He established a glass factory to produce colored glass for windows, lamps, vases, and other objects. He achieved translucent glass of dazzling brilliance. Also he managed to produce different tones in one piece of glass, eliminating the necessity of each tone requiring a separate piece of glass. Tiffany's glass emulated the folds in draped clothing, the shading of flower petals and leaves, the rippling of water, a cloudy sky. He abhorred painting on glass and resorted to it only for facial features.

## What Stained Glass Artists Do

Most artists who work with stained glass these days use glass made by others. The most admired—antique glass—is made in the old way. Machine-made so-called cathedral glass comes in a variety of textures. A milky or marbleized look characterizes opalescent glass. In flashed glass, a layer of colored glass overlays frosted, amber, or clear glass. An artist may etch or sandblast particular areas of a flashed-glass surface to remove the outer layer of glass and so make a design that reveals the contrasting layer beneath.

In traditional stained glass windows or other stained glass objects, strips of lead called *cames* separate the glass pieces and hold them in place. In early days, the makers of stained glass windows made cames by pouring molten lead into hollow reeds. Now an artist buys them ready-made. In cross-section, cames display either an H shape or a U shape. That is, in one type (the H-shaped came) a groove runs along each side with a solid strip between them. The other type (the U-shaped came) has only one groove. The stained glass pieces fit into the grooves of the cames that border them. An artist uses U-shaped cames along outer edges and H-shaped cames everywhere else. Sometimes an artist uses cames of different widths in the same window or object to give variety to the design.

An artist who plans to make a stained glass window or other stained glass object first decides upon a design. One way of arriving at a nonobjective design is to doodle on paper. Sometimes a doodle or part of a doodle, perhaps with modifications, appears suitable for a design. Or an artist might find a design by noticing cracks that make a pleasing pattern in a sidewalk or wall, or the grain of a piece of wood might give an idea for a design. By observing one's surroundings, one can find inspiration in many places.

Usually an artist makes several small designs on paper and colors them, then chooses the most appealing. He or she makes an enlargement of the drawing in the size the finished object is to be in any one of several ways. In one way, the artist draws a grid over the design and on another paper a larger grid that has the same dimensions that the finished work will have. The artist then copies the lines in each square of the small grid onto the matching square of the larger grid, using a correspondingly larger scale.

Taking a photograph of a design and throwing an image of the photograph onto a paper taped to a wall serves as another way of enlarging a design. Moving the projector and adjusting the focus secures an image the proper size. The artist then copies the image on the paper.

The easiest way to enlarge a design is to use a device called a *pantograph*, which is available at art supply stores with directions for its use.

A design in the proper scale is called a *cartoon*. One method of making a leaded-glass window or panel requires two copies of the cartoon. The artist cuts out the shapes on one cartoon using scissors with two cutting edges (available at art supply stores), thereby removing a thin strip of paper between the shapes. The cutaway strips correspond to the spaces the lead cames will fill.

The cutout shapes serve as patterns. The artist fastens a pattern to glass of the right color with a loop of masking tape and then scores the glass around the pattern's edges with a glass cutter. A ruler aids in scoring straight lines; art supply stores stock instruments for cutting circles. The artist separates the scored glass shape from the surrounding glass by tapping the underside of the glass and pulling the glass apart along the scored line.

A light box makes pattern cutting unnecessary. One makes a light box by placing clear glass across the open top of a box and then putting an electric light in the box. The artist indicates on the cartoon the spaces the cames will occupy and positions the cartoon so the shape to be traced lies on the clear glass. The artist then puts glass of the right color over the shape. The light in the box enables the artist to see the outline of the shape through the colored glass. The artist traces the shape on the colored glass with a grease or felt pencil and cuts and detaches the glass in the manner described above.

Before using the cames, the artist stretches them to make them longer by locking one end in a vise and pulling the other end with pliers. After stretching the cames, the artist runs a tool called a *lathekin* down the grooves in the cames to widen the grooves. This operation makes it easier to fit the glass into the lead.

The artist tapes the uncut cartoon to a worktable, nails a strip of wood along one side of the design and another along the bottom, then lays U-shaped cames along the inner edges of the wood strips. The artist fits the pieces of glass that belong on the bottom and side into the U-shaped cames, puts H-shaped cames along the other edges of these pieces, and inserts adjoining pieces of glass into the cames where they belong. If a piece does not fit properly, the artist chips the edges of the glass with grousing pliers to get a good fit. The artist continues in this way, adding glass and cames and occasionally tapping a few nails into the table at strategic points to hold the work in place. When all the glass pieces and cames are in place, the artist nails strips of wood along the top and open side, solders the lead cames at the joints, removes the wood strips, turns the work over, and solders the joints on the other side. He or she works putty under the cames to give strength and to serve as waterproofing. Excess putty is pushed out by pressing the edges of the cames with a lathekin, and as the last step, the work is cleaned, usually by brushing it with whiting, a white powder.

A large work needs an armature, a system of usually vertical and horizontal metal rods. These rods sometimes form a pattern that serves as part of the design.

Modern artists often use copper foil instead of lead cames in making windows and other objects of stained glass. Louis Comfort Tiffany developed this technique. In this method, one crimps strips of foil along the glass edges and bonds adjoining pieces by soldering. This method enables an artist to use intricate designs impossible with the bulkier cames. Also windows of a moderate size or less made with copper foil do not require support rods as leaded windows of comparable size do, nor does copper foil require caulking.

Some modern artists paint details on their glass. Like their predecessors, they paint with enamel and fire the painted glass in a kiln. Sometimes they paint both sides of the glass to reinforce the image.

The use of slab glass that is from seven-eighths of an inch to two inches thick is a modern development. Often slab glass has a rough surface. After cutting slab glass into the needed shapes, an artist usually chips it along its edges with a special hammer, a process called *faceting*. The thickness of slab glass and the faceting give the glass a rugged look. Slab-glass windows and other objects made of slab glass naturally are heavier than they would be if they were made of glass less thick. Consequently they require a framework of either epoxy resin or concrete, either of which gives more support than lead or copper foil does.

To prepare a slab-glass window or other object made of slab glass, the artist tapes the cartoon to a worktable, covers the cartoon with a transparent plastic sheet, assembles the prepared pieces of glass on it in the proper positions, and nails wood strips painted with liquid latex around the perimeter to hold the work in place. The latex coating keeps the epoxy or concrete added later from bonding with the wood.

The artist then pours latex into the channels between the glass pieces—just enough so it seeps under them and forms a thin layer on the undersides of the glass. After the latex dries, the artist pours epoxy or concrete into the channels between the glass pieces. The latex coating prevents the epoxy or concrete from adhering to the undersides of the glass. Sometimes the artist also paints the tops of the glass with latex in case epoxy or concrete spills on them, or both sides of the glass may be painted with latex before assembling. Once dried, epoxy or concrete proves difficult to remove; dried latex pulls off easily.

When epoxy is used, the artist may sprinkle marble chips, sand, or small pebbles on the surface of the epoxy when it is partially dried so as to give it an attractive texture.

When concrete is used, the concrete strips between the pieces of glass must be at least a half-inch wide because concrete is not as strong as epoxy. For a work larger than two feet square, concrete requires internal reinforcement with wire or metal rods.

To achieve a textured surface on the underside of concrete, the artist can place a thin layer of sand, small pebbles, or other material on the plastic sheet that covers the cartoon before positioning the glass pieces. To create a pleasing texture on the upper surface of the concrete, the artist roughens the concrete or presses material into it after the concrete has set for an hour or two.

A stained glass window or other stained glass object constructed with epoxy must lay flat for three or four days after pouring the epoxy to allow the epoxy to cure. If concrete serves as the mortar, the object must remain flat for a week to ten days.

Sometimes an artist creates an attractive glass for a project by laminating pieces of colored glass to clear glass with epoxy on one or both sides. The interplay of light between the layers of glass makes for a richness of color. When using laminated glass, one joins the pieces with dark grout (a thin mortar). The width of a grouted line can vary, making possible delicate and complicated patterns.

An artist who wishes to make a stained glass object other than a window or panel adapts the methods described to the job at hand. For instance, an artist who decides to make a stained glass lampshade will use a plastic-foam, papier-mâché, or fiberglass form to support the work during construction. If using either a plastic-foam or papier-mâché form, the artist applies a coating of gesso (a kind of paste) to the form; after the gesso dries, he or she draws a design on it, makes a copy of the design on tracing paper, and transfers it to a flat drawing. The drawing serves as a pattern for cutting the glass. Using a fiberglass form eliminates one step since fiberglass is transparent. After drawing a design on the fiberglass, the artist puts a light inside the form, places glass on the surface, and marks cutting lines on the glass.

In the past, artists who worked with stained glass mostly constructed windows for churches and homes. Today stained glass windows adorn a wide variety of public buildings as well. This is but one example of the greater opportunities and options open to an artist working with stained glass today. Also, glass comes in a more extensive range of colors than ever before, and an artist can use copper foil, epoxy, or concrete as the framework rather than the traditional lead.

If you become an artist whose medium is stained glass, you will enrich the lives of those who have occasion to view your work at the same time as you build a satisfying career for yourself.

# 21

# Video Art

Video is a relatively new medium for art. While commercial television reaches a wide audience, must please sponsors whose money pays the bills, and must tailor its productions to fit rigid time slots, video art most often appears closed-circuit to a small audience, receives its funding from private sources or grants, lasts for any length of time that seems suitable, and gives attention to any subject the maker desires.

## History of Video Art

Television came into being in the late 1930s. In the early years, an individual or small group could not hope to finance video production because of the high cost of the necessary equipment. A few television stations made studios available to selected artists for limited periods, and grants made possible a few video workshops. Nevertheless, the number of artists who secured access to television equipment remained small. Also, if production took place somewhere besides in a studio, moving the equipment proved a laborious, expensive procedure. Clearly the arrangements for making video art in the early years of television were less than satisfactory.

In 1968 portable, battery-operated, relatively inexpensive video equipment came on the market. As a result many artists began to explore video as an art medium. The production of video art increased tremendously, mainly because video is much more cost effective than film.

A video camera can immediately relay images to a nearby television screen or to a remote location, a feature that gives it an advantage over a camera that uses film, as film requires developing before it can be viewed. A video camera uses the same lenses that a sixteen-millimeter movie camera uses, and an adaptor makes possible the use of thirty-five millimeter still-camera lenses. A videotape recorder when attached to a video camera records the images on tape for later broadcast or for a permanent record. With the proper equipment, one can record images (video) and sound (audio) at the same time. (*Video* is Latin for "to see" and *audio* is Latin for "to hear.") With additional equipment, one can make a film of what the video camera records.

Videotape possesses advantages over film other than not requiring development. Unlike film, one can handle videotape in light. Also, one can erase videotape and reuse it. Night shots impossible with all but the fastest speed of film stock are possible with video.

Just as with film, one can edit videotape. Editing today is done with low-cost digital systems. These digital editing systems can combine still images, film images, computer graphic images, and video in remarkable ways. One exciting aspect of video art is exploring all the possible uses of digital editing.

Like a painting or a photograph, video art has height, width, and the illusion of depth. Unlike a painting or a photograph, however, video art, like a movie, can portray motion and can be accompanied by integrated sound.

## What Video Artists Do

Video artists depict narratives, documentaries, biographical reflections, examinations of the complexities of life, political works, feminist concerns, views of the environment, comedy, dance, visual interpretations of music or poetry, anything at all.

Sometimes the images with which a video artist fills a screen bear no relation to reality. The artist achieves the images by turning the knobs of an electronic synthesizer. A synthesizer is an instrument that brings to the screen dots, lines, and planes in brilliant colors and seemingly in various textures. With these elements, an artist can create a display suggestive of abstract expressionist painting, except that video allows movement and change. A video display generated by a synthesizer sometimes appears similar to a fireworks spectacle; other times the moving elements are more geometrical.

One can use a synthesizer in conjunction with camera images, mixing images from several cameras or combining camera images and synthesized images. Some synthesizers stretch, squeeze, rotate, or reflect both synthesized images and camera images. Some add color to black and white film, add an edge to camera images or change their size, project a negative of a camera shot (dark and light reversed), and/or give a layered look that seems to turn the screen into sculptural space. Some synthesizers activated by sound generate video graphics; others produce sound or alter recorded sound.

Video artists present their works on a single TV monitor or other screen, or on a group of TV monitors and/or other screens. The components of a group may be placed singly, in a horizontal or vertical row, in a pyramid, or any juxtaposition desired.

In a video installation involving more than one screen, each screen may show the same thing, different views of the same thing, or different things entirely. Sometimes the screens show the same thing but with the image in each succeeding screen delayed a few seconds from that on the previous screen. Sometimes a video camera focuses on the audience at an installation and relays images of the audience to monitors. The viewers thus see their own images on the screen.

Nam June Paik, a Korean by birth, was one of the earliest artists to experiment with video and the first person in New York City to buy a portable videotape recorder. He uses his video equipment to explore distortions of video signals, the intermixing of impulses from more than one tape, closed-circuit environments, and video sculptural pieces.

Paik's work has consistently been successful on broadcast TV, no doubt partly because of his ironic humor. In 1970 he presented a four-hour program of synthesized images over Boston's TV station WGBH. The next year the Boston Symphony commissioned a videotape from Paik. While the orchestra played Beethoven's Piano Concerto no. 4 in G Major, Paik's tape showed a large hand battering a small bust of Beethoven. Interspersed shots focused on a flaming toy piano collapsing during a crescendo. In 1972 Paik installed *TV Garden* in a New York gallery, "planting" thirty television sets face up among potted flowers. Strollers in the "garden" watched Paik's videotape *Global Groove* on the upturned sets. This tape features cultural images from around the world. Paik went on to experiment with video images projected by laser beam.

In August of 1993 video artist Inigo Manglano-Ovalle and fifteen of his associates set sixty monitors up along a block of Erie Street on Chicago's West Side. The monitors were set in apartment windows, front yards, and parked cars. Manglano-Ovalle's intent was to display a video portrait of the largely Hispanic neighborhood. This portrait was based mostly on taped interviews with residents of the neighborhood, exploring their memories, the effects of urban development, and the warfare of street gangs on the neighborhood.

In recent years video art has come into its own. Art galleries, art museums, art schools, and video workshops exhibit video art and hold panels and symposia on the subject. Some art museums collect videotapes and hire video curators. Some colleges and universities offer video art programs, some cities boast video workshops, and a few public television stations broadcast works by independent producers and sponsor video artists-in-residence. Magazines devoted to the art have appeared. Interest in video art increases every year.

Anyone wanting to experiment with video as an art medium may find a program devoted to video art in a nearby school or a video workshop in his or her community. Traditional art training as a foundation for later work in video art provides another approach. In this electronic age, artists' use of electronic means to produce art is altogether appropriate.

## Using Your Video-Making Skills

A video artist can use his or her skills in this medium as a means of livelihood. Journalist and producer Janet Gardner heads her own company, The Gardner Group, in New York City. Her company produces videos on subjects as various as Vietnam, the United Nations, and the street gangs of Los Angeles. Her videos are sold in bookstores and to colleges and high schools as well as libraries. Preparation for her present work included going to graduate school at New York University's Institute of Film and Television and working for NBC as a film editor, newswriter, and field producer.

We are all aware of the videotapes of rock stars and other entertainers that are cablecast on TV and of the fantastic advertisements that video artists produce for that industry. There are many TV channels that cablecast, and programming for these channels require a great many producers of video.

The potential for the use of video in classrooms is enormous. If a picture is worth a thousand words, as the saying goes, then video on a specific subject can surely be worth thousands of words. Princeton University, for instance, commissions video artists to produce videotapes that simulate walks through major art museums. These tapes will be invaluable in art history classes.

Companies commission video artists to produce videotapes for the training of their employees and to acquaint potential customers with their services and products. Travel agencies use videotapes to entice potential customers. Video artists also are commissioned to make videotapes of public events like the Olympics or to submit video art to be shown at special events.

An individual might commission a videotape showing his or her estate or home or anything else he or she might desire. Some people commission videotapes featuring a member of their family—say in an interview or showing the family member pursuing his or her usual activities or interests. Different video artists have different styles that they use in this type of portraiture, just as portrait painters have different styles. This use of video carries on the portrait tradition in a new way. Video records of weddings and babies are particularly popular. They can provide employment for videographers just starting out.

Bookstores, in addition to stocking individual videotapes, now have available books that are published with accompanying videotapes. Distributors send out catalogs of available videotapes to individuals on their mailing lists.

Since videotapes can be digitized and fed into a computer, they can be used as part of a computer program. A whole field thus opens to video makers who learn how to interface with computers.

Obviously more and more opportunities are becoming available for those who wish to use their video skills as a means of making a livelihood. According to video artist Paul Ryan of the Graduate Media Studies department of The New School in New York City, "supporting oneself on video art sold through galleries is very difficult. Often video artists get 'day' jobs in the industry to support their work. Increasingly, because of high-quality, low-cost equipment, video artists work as independent producers who succeed in part because they cultivate entrepreneurial skills."

# 22

# WEAVING

WEAVERS CREATE WALL hangings, rugs, coverlets, draperies, table linens, clothing, even sculptures, usually in beautiful glowing colors. Weaving is the interlacing of two sets of threads, most often at right angles to each other. The weaver attaches one set of threads lengthwise on a loom, parallel and equidistant from each other. These lengthwise threads are called the *warp*. The weaver then repeatedly passes crosswise threads from one side of the warp to the other and back, going over some warp threads and under others. These crosswise threads are called the *weft*.

Creativity comes into play in planning the pattern and in choosing the yarns and other materials used. Skill, which comes with practice, enables one to carry the project to completion.

## History of Weaving

Perhaps the earliest weaving occurred when people of the Paleolithic Age wove sticks, vines, and grasses to construct windbreaks and eventually huts. Early people also wove plant fibers into nets for catching fish and carrying things. Out of the need for longer elements to use in making these items came the invention of spinning. Spinning is the drawing out and twisting of plant or animal fibers to make thread or yarn, a necessary prelude to weaving with cotton, wool, or linen. Once people knew how to spin, weaving pliant fabrics followed.

Another prelude to weaving besides spinning is the dyeing of the threads and yarns. In the past, animal, vegetal, and mineral matter were used to give color to these elements. Then chemists devised aniline and other synthetic dyes. As a result, machinery in factories now can dye cloth, as well as spin and weave.

Some hand weavers find satisfaction in doing their own spinning and dyeing. From fennel they secure yellow; from walnut hulls, brown; from onion skins, yellow; from plum leaves, red; from iris blooms, purple; and from plantains, a camel color. These natural sources produce soft luscious hues.

A painting on an ancient Greek vase shows a loom made of two upright poles with a bar across the top. The warp hangs from the crossbar. Weights are attached at the bottom to groups of warp threads to supply tension. Two weavers are weaving from the top down. One person passes a stick with weft threads wound around it through an opening made by inserting a rod horizontally through the warp. Such an opening is called a *shed*. The stick obviously would alternate between going in front of warp threads and then behind warp threads. Modern weavers also create sheds to enable them to pass the weft easily through the warp from one side of the loom to the other, repeatedly going over and then under either single threads or groups of threads separated by a rod. Later weavers fastened the warp to a crossbar at the bottom of vertical looms as well as at the top and wove from the bottom up. When weavers use a vertical loom today, they also work from the bottom up.

Vertical looms have been used and are still used throughout the world. An ancient Egyptian tomb painting shows a weaver with a vertical loom, and Navajo Indians of the American Southwest have used vertical looms for hundreds of years. Navajo weavings were valued trade items as early as the seventeenth century. Traditionally the Navajos created geometrically patterned, boldly colored weavings that they used as blankets. A white man who ran a trading post in Indian territory decided the Navajo blankets would make attractive rugs. He suggested to the Navajos that they make their blankets thicker and then found a ready market among white settlers for Navajo "rugs." Today many view these rugs as desirable wall hangings, and present-day Navajo weavers continue the tradition of their ancestors while responding to modern influences.

Peruvians have been weaving for thousands of years. Paintings on ancient Peruvian pottery show weavers with backstrap looms. The warp on a backstrap loom stretches horizontally between two bars. The weaver ties one bar to a tree or other upright object and fastens the other bar to a strap that goes around the weaver's back. To increase the tension of the warp, the weaver moves forward; to lessen the tension, back. Weavers in South America, Guatemala, Mexico, and remote regions of Asia still use backstrap looms.

The Chinese invented a horizontal loom that consisted of four corner uprights with horizontal braces. They wound the warp around a roller at one end and stretched it horizontally to a roller at the other end. As the length of the weaving increased, they rolled it round the roller in front of the weaver.

For their horizontal loom, the Chinese devised a harness, an arrangement that easily creates a shed. A harness consists of a crossbar suspended above the warp from which heddles hang. Heddles are vertical, parallel cords or wires, each of which has an eye like the eye of a needle at its lower end. The weaver passes warp threads that are to be lifted at the same time through the eyes of a harness's heddles—one thread through each eye—and then passes warp threads to be lifted alternately through the heddle eyes of another harness. The weaver controls each harness with a pedal. When the weaver presses a pedal, the harness it controls rises. Consequently, the threads that pass through the eyes of the harness's heddles rise also, creating a shed. The first looms to use harnesses employed only two. Now more are sometimes used, as many as twelve, depending on the pattern.

Originally the weaver wound the weft around a stick, but now a weaver wraps the weft around a bobbin or shuttle, or sometimes a bobbin fits into a shuttle. When using a small loom, a weaver inserts the bobbin or shuttle into a shed with one hand and draws it out the other side with the other hand. With a larger loom, the weaver throws the bobbin or shuttle through the shed.

A weft thread passed through the warp must be pushed close to the preceding weft thread. A flat stick called a *sword* or *batten* was first used for this purpose. Later someone devised a handheld comblike tool for this purpose. Now looms sometimes come with a comblike arrangement called a *reed* that is the width of the weft and hangs above the work. The spaces between the reed's teeth are called *dents*. When the reed is lowered, one warp thread goes through each dent. A weaver thus beats the full length of a weft row into place with one motion.

After thousands of years of weaving, the fundamentals of the process remain unchanged. By the Middle Ages, the loom used in Europe incorporated the essential features of the loom hand weavers use today.

## What Weavers Do

A small table loom is perhaps the best choice for a beginning weaver. When the weaver becomes more experienced, he or she can purchase a larger loom or build one. Some art supply outlets sell blueprints and instructions for constructing looms.

In plain weave the weft goes repeatedly over one warp thread and then under the next warp thread. On alternate rows the weft goes over the threads it went under in the previous row and under those it went over.

Tapestry weaving, that is, pictorial weaving such as that which produced the Peruvian, Gothic, Renaissance, and Baroque tapestries now in museums, is done with plain weave. In tapestry weaving the weaver, instead of carrying the weft across the width of the warp, carries it back and forth only within an area where a certain color is wanted. The tapestry weaver interlocks the edges of differently colored areas in a variety of ways. One way, of course, is simply to sew adjoining edges together. When making a tapestry, a weaver uses a simple loom, as most mechanical aids must be abandoned. The weaver guides the weft by hand or uses a needle to pull the thread along its path.

In traditional tapestry weaving, the weft completely covers the warp so that the warp isn't visible on the upper surface, a condition accomplished by weaving the weft loosely. When the weaver beats the weft down, the loose threads create "bubbling," which hides the warp.

Basket weave is a variation of plain weave. In basket weave, the weft repeatedly goes over two or more successive warp threads and then under a like number. The weaver follows this scheme for the number of rows that equals the number of warp threads passed over at one time. After the weaver finishes the required number of rows, he or she passes the weft over the warp threads it previously went under and under those it previously went over for the same number of rows as in the previous sequence. The weaver continues this pattern for as long as desired, achieving a checkered look.

Basic weaves besides plain weave are the twill and satin weaves. Twill weave gives a diagonal or zigzag pattern. Satin weave looks and feels smooth because of fewer thread intersections, causing either the weft or warp to predominate on the surface. Leno or gauze weave has a transparent, lacy look. Instructions for creating these weaves can be found in books available at needlework or craft shops.

Through the years weavers have used the weaves described above and other weaves singly or in combinations for carrying out their designs.

A weaver enjoys almost unlimited freedom when he or she makes a wall hanging or sculpture. The weaver may leave some areas devoid of weft with the warp threads exposed, pull some or all weft threads forward between intersections to form loops for a three-dimensional look, or "lay" a design and then surround it with plain weave. To accomplish "laying on," the weaver lifts warp threads to insert threads going in any direction, using a needle to guide the "laid-on" threads.

A woven sculpture represents anything an artist desires and can be any size. Sometimes an armature supports it. A wall hanging or rug might depict a landscape, seascape, other aspects of nature, or a village or city scene. Sometimes wall hangings and rugs picture people from the past or present engaged in a variety of activities. Some artists prefer abstract or nonrepresentational patterns.

Weavers use their imaginations in countless ways to produce beautiful one-of-a-kind scarves, shawls, capes, kimonos, coats, jackets, dresses, blouses, belts, purses, skirts, and anything else for which fabric is suitable.

As a preliminary to weaving, a weaver may sketch possible designs and then enlarge the chosen sketch to the desired size. An enlargement can be made by drawing a grid over the sketch and then on a large paper whose dimensions are those desired for the finished work, drawing a grid with the same number of squares as that of the grid on the sketch. The weaver then copies the portion of the design that is in each square of the small grid onto the corresponding square of the larger grid in a correspondingly larger scale, thus creating the design in the size desired.

The weaver places the enlargement, called a *cartoon*, behind the warp if the loom is vertical, below the warp if the loom is horizontal. The weaver may cut a large cartoon into sections and use one section at a time. The outlines of the cartoon are marked on the warp with a felt marker, brush, or thick pencil. Or one can create a design on a loom either from a mental image or by letting the design evolve as the work progresses.

Once a weaver decides on a design, he or she determines what colors to use, possibly by trying different combinations of colors on small sketches. He or she then purchases the necessary materials and chooses the weaves to use.

Weavers sometimes use materials other than yarns or threads derived from plant and animal fibers. They may include in their weavings strips of fabric, leather, metal, paper, bamboo, or synthetic materials, or they may incorporate ribbons, fringes, roving, beads, ceramic decorations, raffia, feathers, seeds, shells, stones, even dried flowers and leaves. One weaver sometimes uses sewing thread or dyed clothesline; another telephone extension cord and barbed wire! Weavers can introduce virtually anything of a suitable size into their weavings. They can even mix weaving techniques and materials with other media if they believe they are adding to the attractiveness of their work.

The twentieth century brought a renewed appreciation of weaving as an art form. Anni Albers served as a key figure in bringing about this renewed appreciation. She trained in the early part of the century at the Bauhaus, the German school of modern design, then came with her husband, the painter Josef Albers, to the United States at the outbreak of World War II. The couple taught at Black Mountain College in North Carolina, where she inspired several generations of students to create on the hand loom. In 1949 the Museum of Modern Art in New York City gave a one-woman show of her weavings—the first such exhibition to be held there. In the ensuing years, Anni Albers's work became ever more informal. She sometimes used irregular weaves, incorporated a variety of knots into her works, and created designs influenced by ancient weavings. Sometimes she framed her works in glass.

Carole Rae, a San Francisco weaver, creates layered wall hangings as well as ones woven on a single set of warp threads. In her layered wall hangings, she makes some layers of fiber threads, others of narrow strips of transparent, colored Mylar. She weaves frontal layers loosely, so that one sees through them to whatever surprises lie behind. Sometimes Rae incorporates wide strips of irregularly torn dried rag pulp into her weavings. These papers combine rough textures and mixtures of wonderful colors such as soft pinks and roses and tints of blue and green. Rae prepares these papers herself and sometimes places them diagonally with wide spaces between them. Sometimes she encases a wall hanging in a Lucite box.

Handwoven items brighten our environment and find a ready market. Large, glowing, multitextured weavings adorn the interiors of public and corporate buildings. Individuals buy clothing of many types that came from weavers' looms and woven hangings for their homes. The work of some present-day weavers hangs in museums just as the work of their predecessors does.

# 23

# WOODWORKING

SKILLED WOODWORKERS CREATE objects that can be decorative as well as functional. Many people are attracted to woodworking as a hobby. They often set up a workshop in their garage or basement and derive a great deal of pleasure from working with wood.

## History of Woodworking

Through the ages people all over the world have used wood as an art medium. In prehistoric times people carved wooden images of their ancestors and gods. Awe-inspiring wooden figures from ancient Egypt still exist, thanks to the dry climate of the region. The ancient Greeks also carved wooden figures, sometimes of gigantic proportions and oftentimes inlaid or overlaid with precious metals and ivory. Unfortunately, Grecian works of art fashioned from wood did not escape the ravages of time.

In many cultures of the past, artists carved wooden masks for rituals and entertainments and in some areas, in Africa for instance, this practice persists. They also embellished wood posts, lintels, and rafters of houses and meeting places with carvings. They carved designs on wooden staffs, on wooden bowls, and on many other wooden objects used in everyday life and on ceremonial occasions. In Egypt they crafted elegant wooden furniture for the pharaohs. The cache of treasures found in King Tut's tomb contained wooden objects, including furniture. One can see many of these wooden works of art in museums.

In the Middle Ages and throughout the Renaissance, artists carved wooden sculptures for churches and palaces. In England in the seventeenth and early eighteenth centuries, Grinling Gibbons carved wooden panels with flower, fruit, and foliage forms for the homes of the elite and for buildings that were designed by the renowned architect Christopher Wren. Gibbons's artistry in this type of carving is unsurpassed. A revival of this type of carving is now underway.

Early in the twentieth century the Bauhaus, the famous school of art in Germany, decreed that ornamentation was something to be despised, that minimalism and straight lines were to be desired. Now, however, ornamentation is back in favor, and people are appreciating anew the beauty to be found in skillfully carved wood.

In Mill Valley, California, a transplanted Englishman, Ian Agrell, heads The School of Classical Carving, which offers courses in classical carving. Instruction is individual with each student.

## What Woodworkers Do

Today's artist-woodworker uses many kinds of tools. He or she most likely owns chisels, a mallet, scrapers, rasps, and other files. For large pieces of wood, an adze, saws, and planes prove helpful. An adze, a fairly large cutting tool with a blade at right angles to the handle, and saws can serve to rough out a large shape. To use a chisel, a woodworker places its cutting edge against the wood, then maneuvers the chisel so as to make a cut or hits the chisel handle with a mallet so that a chip of wood flies off. A chisel with a curved cutting edge is called a *gouge*. A rasp is a coarse file with cutting points instead of lines, while rifflers are small files and rasps are for working in rounded areas and awkward corners. Tool marks on the surface of wood can make for an interesting texture, or a woodworker may smooth the surface, first with files and rasps, then with sandpaper.

Purists shun power tools, but most artists use power tools for the jobs power tools do best and hand tools for the tasks for which they are best suited. Power tools come in either portable or stationary models. They include saws for cutting, grinders for removing large quantities of wood or for carving designs, drills and routers for hollowing, lathes to rotate a chunk of wood while the artist shapes it with cutting tools, and planers and sanders for smoothing. Types of power saws are reciprocating saws, chain saws, table saws, radial arm saws, band saws, sabre saws, and jigsaws—a considerable variety. Drills and grinders come equipped with bits of various sizes. Bits are biting or cutting parts.

Classes offer a beginning woodworker a chance to try different tools under supervision and to learn how to sharpen and maintain them. Power tools particularly can be dangerous, so a beginner should become familiar with them under the supervision of an experienced woodworker. Knowing how to sharpen a tool properly is of the utmost importance; an instructor can impart this knowledge. After becoming familiar with the capabilities of different tools and acquiring skill in handling them, an aspiring woodworker can then decide which tools to buy.

An artist who plans to make a sculpture of wood either secures a piece of wood and then decides what to do with it or plans a project and then looks for a suitable piece of wood. Lumberyards pro-

vide an obvious source. Better yet are shops that cater to woodworkers. Such shops advertise in art and craft magazines, enabling
an artist to order wood and tools by mail. These shops carry woods
probably never found in a lumberyard as well as familiar ones like
maple, oak, ash, walnut, buckeye, ebony, poplar, pine, and
mahogany. Less familiar woods bear intriguing names like padouk,
cocobolo, siri cote, koa, goncalo alves, zebra wood, amboya, king-
wood, lignum vitae, African black wood, gray harewood, Osage
orange, macadamia, thuya burl, vaquilinia, mesquite, manzanita,
ceanothus, lacewood, English sycamore, toyon, jarrah, albizia
tonna, and guatambu. Many of these woods display attractive figures and colors that an artist can use to advantage.

A figure is the grain pattern revealed when a wood is cut in a
particular manner. Bird's-eye is a commonly known figure that
occurs principally in maple. Attractively figured wood is cut in thin
slices and used for veneering.

Artist-woodworkers particularly prize burl woods for their rich
colors and intricate grain patterns. The source of burl wood is the
hemispheric protuberances that sometimes form on the trunks of
trees as a result of disease. Some artists use the natural cracks and
crevices of burled wood as part of their design. Other attractively
figured wood is found in the crotch of trees, where a tree trunk
divides or a branch grows out from the trunk, or in tree roots.

The less familiar woods have some disadvantages. They may be
expensive, and they sometimes prove very difficult to work with.
Also oils and dust from them may be hazardous to one's health. A
prudent novice seeks advice from a knowledgeable person regard-
ing their use.

Sometimes artists find beautifully weathered wood on beaches
or in forests or secure suitable wood from building wreckers. Some
artists buy furniture from secondhand stores, take the furniture
apart, and use the components in their constructions. Weathered

wood and wood secured from building wreckers and secondhand stores is cured wood; that is, it has been air-dried or kiln-dried.

Tree surgeons, farmers, and builders serve as sources for green wood (freshly cut wood). Cured wood usually cracks less often than green wood, but a large block of cured and unchecked (uncracked) wood is expensive and usually difficult to come by. Green wood frequently sells at a lower price than cured wood and carves easier.

Some artists do not object to cracks and other flaws such as holes, dents, scars, and erosions that are sometimes found in wood; they accept them as natural to wood and believe that they add interest to a work. Other artists fill flaws with splinters or wood filler, so that the repairs are scarcely noticeable.

A woodworker selects wood sufficiently sturdy for the project he or she has in mind and also chooses wood that has attractive color and interesting grain and texture. Wood colors run from almost white through yellow, green, brown, gray, black, red, and purple. A woodworker uses the color of wood to add to the beauty of a work, just as a painter uses the color of paints. He or she also uses the grain to advantage. Cutting wood vertically reveals the grain, whether almost featureless, pin stripes, wide stripes, or intricate. Finished wood presents a variety of textures, like a waxy smoothness or a silky smoothness.

Some artists laminate (glue together) layers of wood to secure a block. Carving laminated wood for a sculpture in the round or in relief reveals the different colors and grains of the layers, which can add to the appeal of a work.

Before they begin to cut wood, most woodworkers form a mental picture of the finished piece they hope to make. If the piece is to be a sculpture, perhaps the shape or grain of the wood suggests an idea. As a preliminary step, some artists sketch on paper, draw on the wood to indicate the form, or make a clay model. Of course, a drawing on wood soon disappears once the work begins, but it gives a start toward the goal.

If a small clay model satisfies the artist, the artist then sometimes makes a clay model the size the finished work will be. A caliper, a measuring instrument with two adjustable legs, transfers dimensions from a full-size model to a block of wood. Some artists dispense with preliminaries; they just begin and let the work proceed according to the inspiration of the moment.

A large piece of wood holds steady by virtue of its weight; otherwise one needs to devise a way of holding the wood still. One can clamp the wood to a workbench or screw it to a swiveling work-positioner attached to a workbench. The latter arrangement allows the artist to work the piece easily from all sides. Or one can lay a large piece of wood across two or more sawhorses held firm by sandbags or tied to a tree or post.

Some artists make three-dimensional wooden sculptures by assembling pieces of wood, perhaps found wood, into pleasing arrangements. (Found wood includes weathered wood, parts of old furniture or wrecked buildings, and scraps left over from other projects.) Or the artist can fashion wood into the components wanted. In either case, the artist joins the components in the desired juxtaposition with glue, nails, screws, corrugated fasteners, or dowels. Such assemblages, unlimited by the dimensions of a log, thrust into space in any manner. Sometimes they incorporate moving parts powered by a motor, a passing breeze, or the viewer. Sometimes they incorporate materials other than wood: iron, glass, plastic, shells, fabric, anything durable.

Types of joints a woodworker uses include the dovetail, scarf, slip or lock corner, bridle, lap and bridle, mortise and tenon, and the doweled joint. Books on cabinetry or joinery explain how to make these joints and other aspects of woodworking. For instance, to countersink a screw, a woodworker drills a hole deep enough so that the screw head drops below the surface of the wood. The artist then fills the space above the screw head with a glued-in plug, either of the same wood and in a manner so as to match the grain or of a different wood for a decorative effect.

A carving done on the surface of a piece of wood so that its forms project from a surrounding more or less flat surface is called a *relief*. Before beginning to carve a relief, an artist usually draws or paints the design on the surface of the wood to serve as a guide, then cuts away the background. In an alternate method, the artist cuts away the wood within the boundaries of the design elements, so that the design recedes below the wood surface, a method called *intaglio*. A design made with grooves, which gives the effect of a line drawing, is an incised design. Relief carving, intaglio, and incising sometimes ornament architectural members such as doors, panels, and lintels or form the design on wooden murals, plaques, trays, trivets, boxes, and furniture.

Some artists make wooden murals or plaques by laminating pre-cut shapes of wood to a wooden background. To get a surface for a large wooden mural, the artist edge-glues planks together. Mounting the mural on the wall is the final step.

In one way of making a print on paper or cloth, the artist prepares a wood surface carved in relief, in intaglio, or incised; rolls printer's ink over the wood surface; then presses unglazed paper or cloth against the inked surface, thus transferring the design carved on the wood to the paper or cloth.

To make rounded wooden objects such as bowls, vases, candleholders, and lamp bases, the artist first roughly shapes the object with a band saw. The artist usually postpones further work for a while to allow the moisture content of the wood to equalize. After a suitable length of time, the artist carves the piece to its final form on a lathe.

## Using Your Woodworking Skills

Bowls have been made from wood since ancient times, but it is only in the last few decades that the idea that a bowl can be considered a work of art rather than just a utility item has emerged. The beauty of the wood chosen for a bowl contributes to its appeal as well as the artist's skill in shaping the wood.

Some artist-woodworkers let their imaginations run free in the realm of toys. One artist produced a knobby, undulating worm on rockers as a substitute for the usual rocking horse.

Some woodworkers specialize in furniture. They create chairs, settees, stools, tables, buffets, desks, chests, cabinets, beds, cradles, music stands, dictionary stands, library steps, and any other type of furniture they think of. Some artists' furniture harks back to primitive times by assuming a crude look, perhaps with bark left on the wood. Other furniture made by artists reflects the simplicity of Early American, Shaker, or modern Scandinavian design. Still other artist-made furniture seems completely original. Sometimes artist-made furniture has some parts that are made of metal, plastic, marble, leather, or lacquerwork.

Sometimes artists who make furniture of wood steam wood in a press, a process that makes it possible to bend wood into curved shapes.

Some artists produce whimsical furniture: a chair in the shape of a hand or a seated person, a chest of drawers set into the torso of a "human," bookshelves that look like a man's jacket, with books in evidence only in the V between the lapels. In the latter case, "unbuttoning" the jacket (that is, unfastening a latch) and opening the doors that form the jacket's front reveals more books and shelves.

After arriving at an idea for a piece of furniture, an artist draws plans and sometimes makes a scale model. Wood selection comes next: hardwood, plywood, particleboard, or fiberboard. The artist covers the latter three with veneers of exotic hardwoods, leathers, or plastics. Plywood, particleboard, and fiberboard offer the advantage of being impervious to the contracting and expanding brought on in hardwoods by variations in humidity.

Modern technology provides new methods of constructing furniture. An artist takes advantage of these methods when they suit the purpose, as using machines to give a smooth, flawless surface and to make joints invisible. Contrarily, some artists prefer a rough-hewn look and exposed joints.

Just as a printmaker numbers prints pulled from the same design, a furniture maker sometimes makes editions (that is, a limited number) of a furniture design and numbers and signs each piece.

The late George Nakashima ranked among the best of the artists making furniture in the United States. A Japanese-American working in the village of New Hope in the hills of eastern Pennsylvania, Nakashima involved himself with the entire process of creating beautiful furniture, starting with the very basics in the selection of trees and the first rough cutting of logs. He preferred to work with nature rather than impose his will upon it. He prized the natural color, grain, burl, and organic forms of wood and used them to supreme advantage. Nakashima's coffee tables in particular, which he made from slices of the trunk or roots of redwood or English walnut, brought him much fame. At least five thousand artist-woodworkers in the United States currently are engaged in creating handmade furniture.

The final step in any type of woodworking is treating the wood to protect it from dust and deterioration. Shellac, wax, and oil act as preservatives without changing the color. Shellac also keeps dust from penetrating. Several coats of wax bring out the grain.

Paints, dyes, and inks color wood as well as protect it. Stains color without obscuring the grain. Wood bleach lightens it. Working with wood brings special satisfactions. The glow of wood smoothed and polished is lovely to behold, while cuts made in the wood by the chisel may reflect the light like a diamond. Caressing the smoothness of a wood finish or following the grain of wood or the curves of wood carving with one's fingers brings sensuous pleasure. In addition, wood often gives forth a wonderful aroma. Rosewood gets its name because when freshly cut it gives off an aroma like that of roses. The fact that wood once constituted part of a living organism also adds to the appeal of working with wood. An artist creating with wood gives it a new life in a different form.

A woodworker who is an artist may draw inspiration from historical furniture styles, architecture, industrial design, folk art, mixed media, or other sources.

## How to Get Started in Woodworking

Many people learn woodworking skills in high school or college. Anyone wishing to qualify as an artist-woodworker needs more than woodworking skills, however. Such a person also needs a good sense of design. For that reason many aspiring woodworkers study art and furniture design in colleges, universities, and art schools. There they learn how to use line, mass, shape, texture, and color to secure results that please the eye.

Some woodworkers get their training by serving as apprentices to master woodworkers. The aforementioned carver Ian Agrell, who carves architectural elements and furnishings, accepts students for a two-day weekend class or a five-day weekday class. Books also can serve as teachers for aspiring woodworkers.

In San Francisco, the Sheridan Studio offers classes in beginning and advanced woodworking. John Sheridan, the owner, who is a respected furniture designer and teacher, says students should be serious about making a long-term commitment (one to two years) to learning the skills of woodworking.

# 24

---

# IDEAS TO GET YOU STARTED

MANY OF THE art and craft ideas described in this book can be learned on one's own, perhaps with the aid of a book. In most instances, however, you can get a more thorough grounding and exposure to your particular interest—not to mention the important credentials—by attending classes at a technical school, college, or university that offers the appropriate courses. Barron's publication *Profiles of American Colleges*, which is generally available at public libraries, lists colleges and universities that offer majors in some of the arts and crafts discussed in this book.

Some other avenues you can consider include the following:

- Become an apprentice to someone already a master at what you wish to learn.
- Find out if there are communal workshops available to artists in your field where you can find facilities, supplies, and like-minded individuals who will inspire you and help you get the skills you need.

- Check out YMCAs, YWCAs, art schools, community centers, city recreation departments, senior citizens centers, professionals willing to give private instruction, and other options in your community.

There are many options open to those who would like to make a living or start a business working on a particular art or craft:

- Check with employment agencies to see if there are openings for artists or craftspeople with your particular skills.
- Make arrangements with an art gallery or gift shop to sell your work on consignment.
- Open an art gallery with other artists where you can display and sell your wares.
- Find out if your town has a cooperative gallery where artists and craftspeople offer their works for sale.
- See if owners or managers of businesses—hospitals, corporations, clinics, beauty shops, doctor's offices, fitness centers, restaurants, and so forth—would like to display your work on their walls or premises. A small label on a bottom corner of each item could give your name and the price of the artwork on it. This would be beneficial to businesses as your work would enhance their environment. Note that the owners or managers may want a commission on sales.
- Look in the Yellow Pages of your telephone directory for organizations that sell the type of art you produce.
- Display and sell your work at art fairs.
- See if friends and acquaintances who admire your work would like to purchase something.
- If applicable, advertise in magazines.

- Send out mailings, distribute flyers, ask friends and acquaintances to spread the word about you.
- Open a shop or studio in your home, if local law permits.
- Check out mail-order companies if you wish to produce in multiples. Answer ads for employment or for commissions for the type of work you do.

# About the Author

Elizabeth B. Gardner, better known as Betty, was born and grew up in Edwardsville, Illinois. She graduated with a Bachelor of Arts degree from MacMurray College in Jacksonville, Illinois. She now lives in San Francisco with her husband, one of their three daughters, and their cat, Max. She was a docent at the Dayton Art Institute and then at The Fine Arts Museums of San Francisco for many years.